Modern Railways

SPECIAL

CW01668049

TGV

Brian Perren

Published by

IAN ALLAN LTD

Coombelands House Weybridge KT15 1HY

Telephone: Weybridge (0932) 858511

Printed by Ian Allan Printing at their works at Coombelands in Runnymede, England

First published 1988

ISBN 0 7110 1706 9

Published by Ian Allan Ltd, Shepperton, Surrey; and printed by Ian Allan Printing Ltd at their works at Coombelands in Runnymede, England

Front cover:
The marketing and image of the TGV service has been helped by the striking end design of the units. *SNCF*

Back cover, top:
Paris Gare du Lyon plays host to two TGV units on 26 July 1982. *C. M. Whitehouse*

Back cover, bottom:
A Postal TGV unit speeds through the French countryside. *SNCF*

1. A Technical and Market Base

Today few would deny that French Railways (SNCF) operates the most technologically-advanced, efficient and market-conscious railway network in Europe, if not the world. Pride of the system is the high speed *Train à Grande Vitesse* (TGV) running over the new purpose-built railway (the *Ligne à Grande Vitesse* or LGV) at speeds of up to 270km/hr (167.8mph) which links Paris with the city of Lyon in a mere 2hr at a start-to-stop average speed of 214km/hr (132.7mph).

The building of the TGV has to be viewed against the French political environment. During the past 15 years or so, successive French Governments — be they of the left or right — have supported high investment in the revitalisation of the nation's infrastructure. Modernisation of the SNCF is part of a national plan which has transformed the telephone system, created a modern motorway network, improved urban public transport, built new airports and has converted the nation's electricity supply industry to nuclear generation.

Although the decision to build the new Paris-Sud Est line (TGV-PSE) was made by the French Government in January 1977, the project evolved from many years of research and technical development. Today, although only 29% of the SNCF network is equipped for electric working, 83% of its traffic is moved by electric traction. While all recent electrification in France has used the more efficient and cheaper 25kV ac system, a large part of pre- and postwar electrification was carried out at 1,500V dc. As the cost of converting 1,500V dc catenary and fixed equipment to 25kV ac cannot be justified, a large fleet of dual and multi-voltage locomotives and EMUs have been built for universal working throughout France.

In the 1950s, given the funds for new main line electrification and an influx of new equipment offering scope for higher speeds and heavier loads, a programme of research was initiated to obtain data for future design work. The purpose was to determine the performance of conventional electric locomotives, the behaviour of rolling stock,

the efficiency of current supply systems and the ability of fixed electrification equipment to cope with the heavy voltage consumption necessary for the maintenance of high speeds or the haulage of heavy loads. Included in the programme was a series of very high speed test runs culminating in a world record speed of 331km/hr (205.6mph) which remained unchallenged until a new maximum speed of 380km/hr (236.1mph) was established by TGV unit No 016 on 26 February 1981.

The development of ac power supplies for traction purposes and the testing of track, fixed electrification equipment, locomotives and rolling stock for very high speeds produced outstanding technical achievements. They created a solid technical base which enabled SNCF to develop its railway business and the French railway equipment industry to capture a large share of the world railway export market.

A wider market base

It used to be said that, while SNCF was the leading technical railway in Europe, British Rail was the leader in marketing skills. But by the end of the 1960s the change in market environment led SNCF to reappraise its entire passenger business strategy. The reasons for these changes and SNCF's response to the new age of the mass travel market is an important element in the development of TGV.

Given the success of its technical research, SNCF's attitude to the practical application of higher rail speeds as a commercial selling point was in retrospect cautious. Twelve years were to elapse before the first public service timed to run at speeds up to 200km/hr (125mph) would be launched. However, staging one-off high-speed spectaculars, in a controlled situation over a section of railway closed to all other

Far left:
BB9004 on its record-breaking run on 29 March 1955 when it achieved a record speed of 331km/hr (205.6mph). *SNCF*

A postwar problem in Europe was the development of several different systems of power supplies for rail traction. While the SNCF decided to adopt 25kV for all future projects, the cost of converting the existing 1,500V dc network could not be justified. To facilitate locomotive utilisation, locomotives were designed to cope with ac and dc systems both within France and in neighbouring countries such as Belgium and Switzerland. The first of the SNCF series of multi-voltage locomotives was the 40100 class Co-Co designed to cope with four different voltages. *Below:* **Co-Co No 40101 arrives in Paris Nord with an express from Brussels. The Swiss also developed a very successful four-voltage train. This is the type RAe TEE EMU for through workings between France, Switzerland and Italy,** *Left:* **one of these units approaches Blaisy Bas on the PLM main line with the Paris to Milan 'Cisalpin' TEE. Today the 'Cisalpin' TEE and other services to Lausanne in Switzerland have been replaced by three-voltage TGV units which work to Lausanne and Berne.** *(Both) SNCF*

Above:
At first SNCF used its high-speed technology to meet the upper end of the market. The first train to run at 200km/hr (125mph) was the Paris-Toulouse 'Capitole' TEE. This picture shows the train hauled by CC No 6523 shortly after it had been re-equipped with 'Grand Confort' stock. *SNCF/Broncard*

traffic, is clearly not the same as running 200km/hr (125mph) services where these trains have to cohabit with other slower moving trains on a routine day-to-day basis.

SNCF's policy was to make haste slowly. The first priority was safety. Further technical research was directed towards the design and development of new signalling devices, the elimination of level crossings, the strengthening of track and bridges, the easing out of curves and the enhancement of vehicle braking performance. For some years the maximum permitted line speed on French trunk routes was 150km/hr (93.2mph), but this was raised to 160km/hr (100mph) on sections of the Paris-Lyon-Mediterranée (PLM) main line in 1965.

Operating and commercial policy specified the progressive acceleration of all passenger services with particular emphasis on the efficient haulage of (by British standards) very big trains of 16-17 vehicles often grossing 800 tonnes. The outstanding feature of French intercity train speeds during the 1960s was that average speeds were timed at levels very close to the maximum line speed.

SNCF's first public service to be timed at speeds of up to 200km/hr (125mph) was introduced with the start of the summer timetable in May 1967. The trains involved were the evening First Class-only 'Capitole' business services in each direction over the 713km (443 miles) between Paris and Toulouse. As essential prerequisite of the 'Capitole' operation was the introduction of a new signalling system designed for high speed running. Clearly the cost of re-equipping complete sections of trunk routes with a new signalling system capable of controlling all traffic irrespective of speed, was a cost the SNCF was not prepared to meet. The preferred solution was a compromise whereby the existing signalling was augmented by a visual display in the driving cab.

Encouraged by the success of the 'Capitole' which quickly built up new custom, SNCF decided to extend 200km/hr services to the Paris-Bordeaux route. New equipment — Class 6500 Co-Co locomotives and 'Grand Confort' coaches — capable of 200km/hr speeds was built. These services were incorporated into the Trans-Europe Express (TEE) First Class-only network, but by the start of the 1970s this market started to decline.

'Corail' opens the mass market

By the start of the 1970s, other major railways in Europe — with British Rail leading the field — were beginning to realise the vast potential of the newly developing mass travel market which had gathered momentum in the second half of the 1960s. Jet aircraft had created the package tour and the growth of private car ownership had given people a new sense of mobility

Table 1: 'Corail' Coach Orders 1975-1985

Type	*1975*	*1978*	*1980*	*1982*	*1983*	*1984*	*1985*	*Cumulative total*
Open Compartment	1,300 845*	674 254	147 199	110 —	— 65	— 30	— 26	2,231 1,419
Total	2,145	928	346	110	65	30	26	3,650

*Includes 100 VSE (Voiture Standard European) Comparment Firsts

The 'Corail' Revolution

Above:
In the mid-1970s — faced with a long-term decline in Second Class ticket sales — SNCF decided to revamp their marketing efforts and enter the mass travel market. Train services were recast, stations refurbished, new market initiatives launched and a fleet of over 3,000 new air-conditioned coaches were brought into service. Marketed under the brand name 'Corail' the new trains were a great success and attracted new traffic. The 'Corail' services paved the way for TGV. The photograph shows a typical rake of 'Corail' stock hauled by a Class 7200 Bo-Bo No 7279 at Aix-les-Bains in the French Alps. *SNCF/Broncard*

Left:
Recognising the importance of the mass travel market, SNCF initiated a major renewal of its long-distance passenger vehicle fleet with new air-conditioned 'Corail' coaches. This 'Corail' formation has just arrived at Paris-Austerlitz from Bordeaux. *SNCF/Demoy*

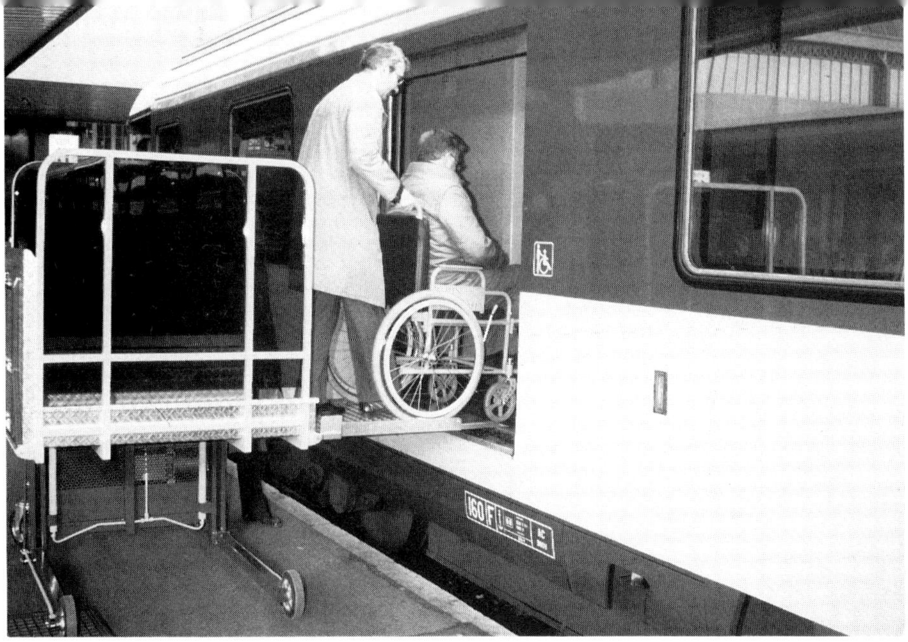

and social freedom. Selling mobility had tremendous potential for rail. British Rail soon found that a good baseload of optional business was essential for survival.

InterCity took off in the late 1960s because they had a good product which was effectively marketed. Impressed by British Rail's results, SNCF decided they too had a future in the mass market. By the end of the 1970s the image of the SNCF had been entirely transformed. New market-led timetables, which were designed with less emphasis on the previous practice of running groups of trains at traditional departure times, were introduced to tap business. Station facilities — another source of complaint — were vigorously tackled. In some cases new stations were funded through joint ventures undertaken with outside commercial companies — Lyon Part-Dieu is a case in point.

The most significant contribution to the expansion of SNCF's business was the new fleet of 'Corail' coaches. Market research had enabled SNCF to build up a basic idea of the types of vehicle they would need for the contemporary travel market. The specification catered for a good general ambience, good riding characteristics and effective sound insulation — full air conditioning was considered essential. After the testing of prototype vehicles, SNCF obtained Government approval for a rolling programme of vehicle construction.

Looking back after 10 or more years, the sheer scale of the 'Corail' project is still impressive ('Corail' — by the way — is a contraction of 'Comfort' and 'Rail'). The 1975 and 1978 orders provided for a total of 3,073 coaches which were followed by another 346 ordered in 1980. By then vehicle acquisition had switched over to the PSE TGV fleet, but small numbers of 'Corail' coaches have been subsequently built — the majority being specialist vehicles such as couchette cars. 'Corail' trains were very well received by the French public to the extent that a healthy growth in business was rekindled. The importance of the 'Corail' fleet in revitalising French rail travel in the second half of the 1970s should not be underestimated. It revived public interest in rail as an acceptable contemporary travel mode and in so doing prepared the French public for the TGV.

Above left:
A mobile, electrically powered, hydraulic lift is provided to enable a wheelchair-bound passenger to gain access to a 'Corail' vehicle. *SNCF/CAV*

Below:
The new fleet included a new design of catering car — the 'Bar Corail'.
SNCF/Dewolf

2.

The Paris-Sud Est Line

Successful though they were — and of course still are — SNCF never regarded its group of 200km/hr (125mph) locomotive-hauled trains (which now total 40 or so) as anything other than a stop-gap commodity. Their long-term aspirations were aimed at much higher commercial speed maximum. However, the Toulouse, Bordeaux and Nantes services were a necessary and successful commercial initiative to meet specific markets. The Sud-Ouest TEEs held rail's share of the Bordeaux-Paris business market in the face of competition on Air Inter and 'Corail 200' was a necessary response to the threat to optional First and Second Class business posed by the new A10 'Aquitaine' autoroute. On the Paris-Nantes route the local authority was prepared to meet part of the cost of equipping the Le Mans-Nantes line for 200km/hr (125mph) running.

SNCF's long-term high-speed strategy was crystallised during the second half of the 1960s. Two important factors prevailed. Technical research and testing had shown that very high speeds on certain trunk routes were possible, but could only be achieved by costly track and signalling modifications and with unacceptable loss of route capacity. Experience had shown that higher train speeds could attract a larger market share, but to be competitive on long-haul routes a top speed in the range of 250-300km/hr (155-185mph) would be necessary. Such speeds could only be achieved by the provision of separate purpose-built high-speed tracks for the exclusive use of passenger trains. Lastly, given that route capacity *per se* was likely to be a long-term constraint for both passenger and freight traffic, the construction of new passenger tracks enabling passenger and freight trains to be segregated was a more cost-effective proposition. Thus SNCF's planners started work on tentative plans for a network of new high-speed railways radiating out from Paris to Provincial France. The routes were Paris-Sud Est, TGV-Nord to Lille, the Channel Tunnel, Brussels, Amsterdam and West Germany and TGV-Atlantique to West and South-West France. TGV-PSE was SNCF's first priority. Had the British Government gone ahead with the Channel Tunnel in the 1960s, TGV-Nord would have been seen as the second project with TGV-Atlantique third. When the British withdrew from the Channel Tunnel project in the early 1970s, TGV-Nord was replaced by TGV-Atlantique as the second priority.

Detailed planning of the TGV-PSE started in the late 1960s, but the project was not declared a 'Public Utility' until March 1976. Under French legislation, a major public project such as the TGV has first to be declared by the Government who then hear objections from interested parties. Final confirmation as a 'Public Utility' followed in January 1977. Work then started.

SNCF's traffic forecasts had identified a long-term capacity problem on its premier Paris-Lyon-Mediterranée (PLM) route. The PLM is France's most famous and important trunk route linking Paris, Dijon, Lyon, the Rhône Valley and Marseille. It makes important international connections with Switzerland and Italy and serves 40% of the entire population of France. With a growth rate of about 4% per year, the time was foreseen when the route would be saturated to the extent that SNCF's ability to cope with its basic passenger and freight business would be impaired. The capacity problem was twofold. While a large proportion of the 315km (196 miles) of route from Paris to Dijon was four-tracked, two critical two-track sections — St Florentin to Les Laumes (83km/52 miles) and Blaisy Bas to Dijon (26km/16 miles) — made it extremely difficult to cope with a mixture of heavy freight services and 100mph passenger trains.

The second restricting feature on the PLM was line speed. In contrast to the Paris-Bordeaux route — which had been upgraded for high speeds at a very modest outlay — the topography of the PLM was such as to rule out any major line speed improvements. For example, the prospect of doubling the Blaisy Bas Tunnel (4km/2.5 miles) and realigning the two-track section down the valley to Dijon was simply not a practical proposition. Thus, even though the route had only been electrified for a little over 10 years, its practical maximum operating capacity was within sight.

Given the impracticalities of upgrading the PLM, plans were prepared for a new high-speed railway which would bypass it. The cost of upgrading the PLM (where this was possible) was equal to 40% of the cost of the proposed alternative. Moreover, by using all the resources and knowledge of modern rail technology, the cost of the new infrastructure would be considerably less than traditional methods. Despite the fact that the new railway passes through some very hilly areas of France there are no tunnels. It has been constructed like a motorway. Trains on the new railway, which has been built to a maximum railway gradient of 35%, simply go up and over the hills. Naturally, such a demanding gradient profile calls for a very high level of traction power output.

Paris to Lyon — the new route

Many people have the impression that the TGV is a self-contained high speed system; this is not so. While the new railway — now generally referred to as the Ligne à Grande Vitesse (LGV) — is only equipped to carry TGVs and a few specially equipped locomotive-hauled maintenance trains, it is part of the French national network and the TGV units themselves are technically capable of working over any line which is electrified.

In the case of the Paris-Sud Est TGV, the only way by which the trains could reach the centres of Paris and Lyon was to use the existing railway network. At the time of its construction there was no way that SNCF could either meet the cost or face the environmental upheaval of taking new tracks through the Paris suburbs. TGVs would therefore start from and terminate at the Gare de Lyon — the largest terminal station in the city. But, as was also the case at Lyon, major works in the Gare de Lyon area were necessary.

To cope with the increase in frequency, in-and-out platform working,

and provide new expanded passenger reception areas, the Gare de Lyon and its approaches have been completely remodelled. Hitherto, the station had been divided into separate main line arrival and departure sections, separated by commuter platforms in the centre. Commuter trains could turn round in the platforms, but all main line trains were taken out to Conflans carriage depot and worked back to the departure side after cleaning. SNCF were looking for a 45min turnaround for a TGV set and this called for a set of dedicated platforms. So, as part of long-term plans for the Paris area suburban services, a new four-platform sub-surface station was built for the commuter trains. This was completed in 1982, releasing space in centre of the station for a group of five special TGV platforms for in-and-out working. Each is capable of holding two 2+8 TGVs which between them occupy a total track length of 400.2m or 436yd. These platforms have inspection pits for the carrying out of routine checks between trips. Another feature of the revamped Gare de Lyon is the new sub-surface TGV departure area, which is located under the original departure platforms and includes booking and reservation offices, shops, cafes and bars.

Beyond the station platforms a modified track layout has been installed and resignalled. To handle the extra traffic between the Gare de Lyon and Lieusaint (the start of the new railway) additional block sections have been

Below:
A diagram illustrating the principal installations at the Paris end of the PSE route, showing the relative positions of the Gare de Lyon, Bercy-Conflans Depot and the Villeneuve workshops.

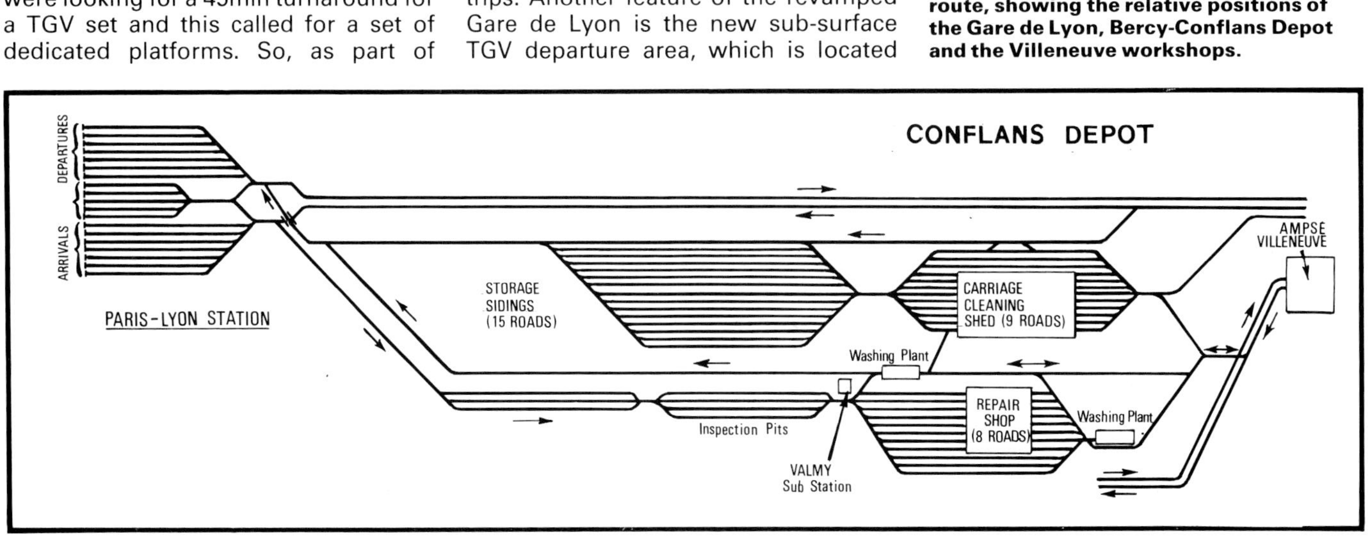

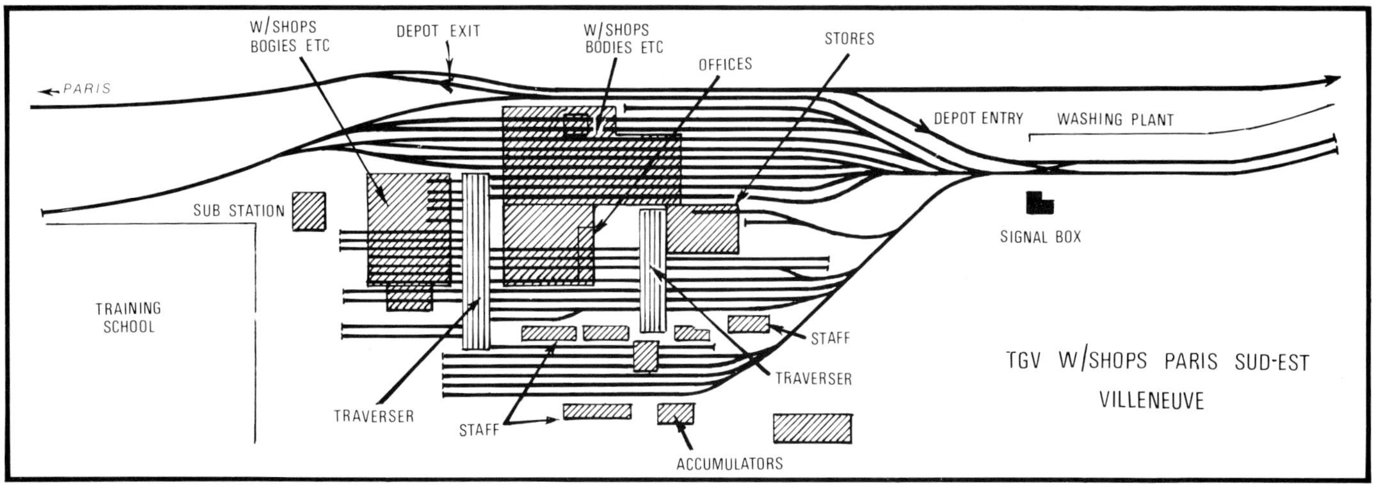

Above:
Track plan of the Villeneuve workshops.

Left:
To cope with the extra business which will be generated by TGV, the Gare de Lyon at Paris had to be substantially remodelled. To provide more capacity in the main station, a new sub-surface group of platforms was built to accommodate Sud Est suburban trains. This picture shows the new sub-surface station in the course of construction; the main Gare de Lyon platforms are to the right of the picture. *SNCF*

installed. Just outside the station, Conflans Depot, previously used by locomotive-hauled stock, has been modified for TGV servicing and cleaning. A new major maintenance depot for the entire TGV fleet, known as Paris Sud Est Depot, has been built at Villeneuve.

The LGV starts at a new junction at Lieusaint, 29km (18 miles) out of Paris on the PLM main line and ends at Sathonay in the northern outskirts of Lyon. In addition to these two connections, the LGV has three other junctions. The first is at St Florentin, the second at Aisy and the third at Mâcon. From September 1981 until September 1983, the junction with the PLM at St Florentin (Verigny) was the temporary end of the new line pending completion of the northern part of the LGV. St-Florentin is now an emergency link with the PLM. The short 15.2km (9.5 miles) branch from Aisy to Pasilly is the route for TGVs from Paris to Dijon, destinations in Eastern France and Switzerland. At Mâcon there is a further series of junctions with the PLM and the important route through Bourg-en-Bresse which leads to the Savoy Alps, Geneva and the Mont Cenis route to Turin in Italy.

Mention should be made of the short spur to and from the Chagny branch at Montchanin. Originally built as a means of access for construction works, it is now used for permanent way and catenary maintenance trains. A remarkable feature, compared with British conditions, is the provision of only two intermediate stations. These are at Le Creusot, which serves the industrial town of Montchanin, and Mâcon. This situation is typical of France where the population is spread over a very wide geographical area.

Below:
The Gare de Lyon after remodelling. The former suburban platforms are now used by TGVs. *SNCF/Michel Herin*

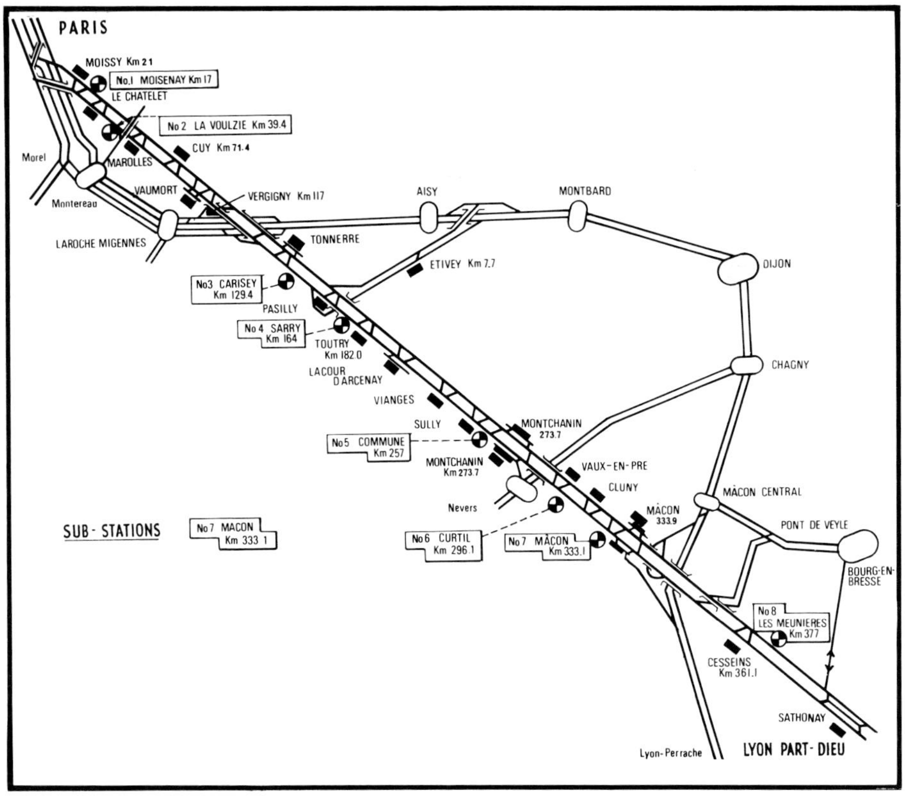

Above:
Route diagram of the PSE route showing the track layout, junctions, electrical sub-stations and signal relay posts.

Above:
TGVs awaiting departure from the Gare de Lyon. The station clocktower, a well known Paris landmark, is in the background. *SNCF/CAV*

As mentioned the LGV starts at Lieusaint, 29.4km (18.27 miles) from the Gare de Lyon at Paris. Originally, the start point of the new line was given as Combs-la-Ville, but in the event the junction was located at Lieusaint. The Combs-la-Ville signalbox control area has now been merged with that at Lieusaint where a new panel controls the junction. From the Gare de Lyon to Lieusaint (and beyond) the PLM is four-tracked. As can be seen from the plan, from Paris to Lieusaint the tracks are paired by use — Nos 1 and 2 are fast and Nos 1b and 2b are relief — but beyond Lieusaint they are paired by direction. Built to connect the PLM with the LGV, the new double flyover carries the LGV line over Tracks Nos 1, 1b and 2 to join track 2; the connection between LGV track 2 and PLM 2 is made on the flyover. Line speed on all four tracks — including the flyover and junctions — is 160km/hr (100mph). The voltage changeover from dc to ac is just on the new line.

From Lieusaint, the LGV runs straight out into open country in the Department de Seine-et-Marne. To optimise construction costs the first few miles of route have been built on a common infrastructure with a proposed new A5 motorway. This is across the plain of Brie — famous for its cheese production — passing near to but carefully avoiding (for environmental reasons) the towns of Melun, Montereau and Sens.

At St Florentin (Verigny), which is 117km (73 miles) from Lieusaint, the line splits to cross the PLM on two separate single-track bridges. This spacing out of the layout is to provide for the 160km/hr (100mph) spurs connecting the PLM (Paris direction) to the LGV (Lyon Part-Dieu direction). As mentioned earlier, for the first two years of TGV working this was the northern end of the LGV, but these two connections are now for emergency purposes only. Beyond St-Florentin the LGV becomes more interesting. Passing near to the town of Connerre, the line soon reaches the flying junction at Pasilly. Designed to be taken at 220km/hr (137mph), the layout is spread over a considerable distance. Now in the Côte d'Or, the line begins to pass through the Burgundy hills, with fine scenic views of the Morvan natural park. It is in this area that one starts to notice the variable, switchback nature of the roadbed. Le Creusot station, in the Department de Saône-et-Loire, is 273.8km (170 miles) from the start of the LGV. From here to Mâcon (333.4km/207 miles) the line follows an undulating course to Kilometre Post (KP) No 315 where the route starts a 35% climb for 5km (3.1 miles) up to the 3,500m summit at Col du Bois Clair, from where a rapid descent is made down to Mâcon-Loché TGV station. Speed over the summit is restricted to 220km/hr (137mph). A feature of the railway here is the short common alignment with the RN79 trunk road.

Mâcon — the well-known Burgundy wine town — is an important point on the LGV. Mâcon-Loché TGV station, which is about three miles from the town, is located a few minutes' drive from the Maconnais and Beaujolais vineyards. The station has two long loop platforms, both of which are

Below:
As well as making the connections between the PLM tracks and the TGV, the Lieusaint junction layout also changes the position of the PLM tracks which are paired by direction south of the junction.

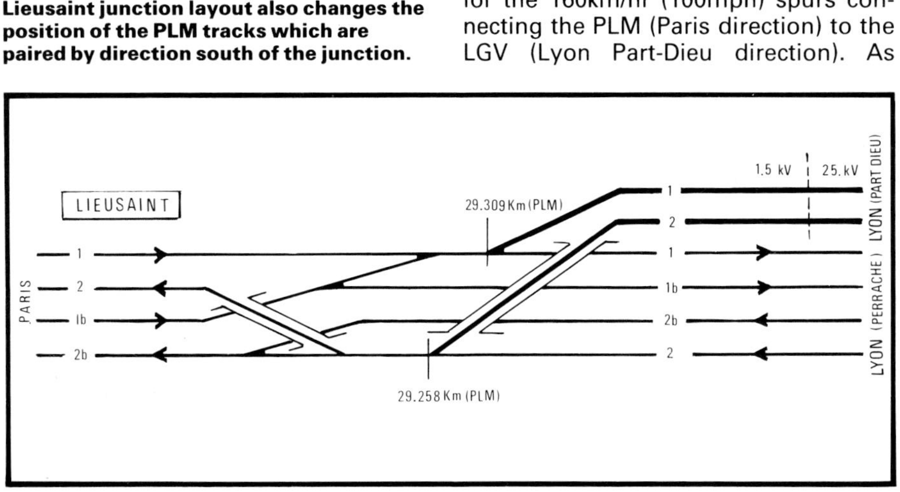

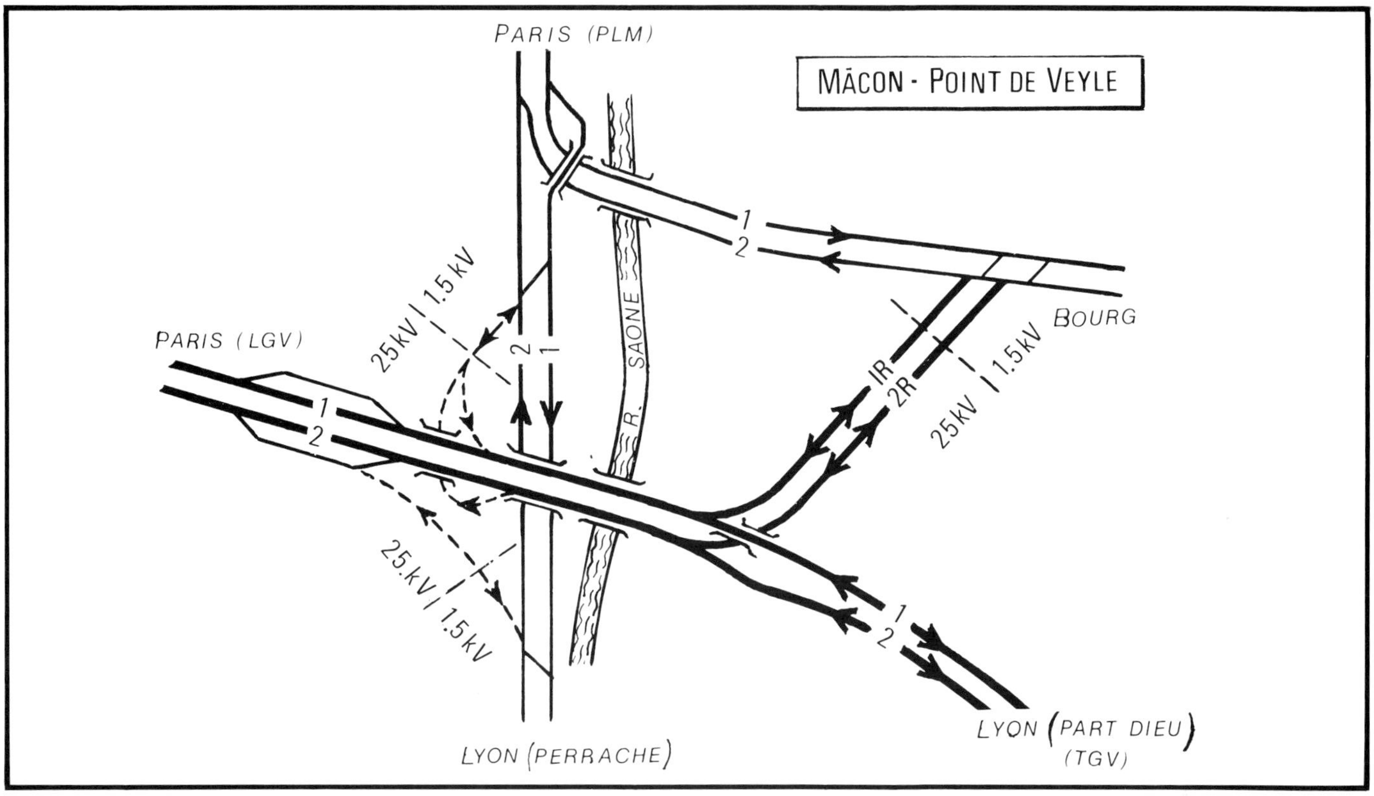

Above:
Mâcon is the junction between the LGV and the branch to Bourg and the Savoy Alps. Emergency links with the PLM line and Mâcon's postal station are also provided.

signalled for reversible working, with the through roads in the centre. There is a large car park and a connecting bus service to the towns of Villefranche and Belleville which is operated by SNCF. There is an important series of junctions. Immediately south of the station's northbound platform is a single-line link round to the PLM main line which passes under the LGV beyond the TGV station; Mâcon Vinzelles TGV postal depot is located on this spur. The Postal TGV is the only regular working on this link, which is also an important emergency line. There are additional emergency lines from the LGV (Lyon direction) round to the PLM (Paris direction). Finally, after

Below:
Routine servicing and cleaning of TGVs is undertaken at Paris Bercy-Conflans Depot which is close to the Gare de Lyon.
David Haydock

the LGV crosses the viaduct over the River Saône, there is the junction and flyover at KP337 for the Bourg-en-Bresse line. This high-speed junction, which is used by TGVs to Geneva and the Savoy Alps, joins the original PLM line from Mâcon-Ville at Pont-de-Veyle. The distance from the LGV junction to Pont-de-Veyle is 7.6km (4.72 miles) and is 7.7km (4.78 miles) from Mâcon-Ville PLM station. TGVs from Paris to the Bourg line not stopping at Mâcon-Loché have to reduce speed to 160km/hr for the junction at Pont-de-Veyle. A voltage changeover is also necessary.

In contrast to the rest of the route, the final 30 miles or so through Department de L'Ain to Sathonay passes fairly easy country with no gradients of any significance. At Sathonay, TGVs enter the Lyon urban area. TGVs terminating at Lyon first call at the new Part-Dieu station, prior to terminating at Lyon Perrache. SNCF are to be congratulated on the way they have carried out the course of the new railway with the absolute minimum of interference with their natural amenities.

Above:
A TGV bound for Paris comes off the LGV over the flyover at Lieusaint and crosses a suburban EMU heading out of Paris.

Below left:
A view of the line, showing its gradients, south of Pasilly; a two-unit TGV forms a Paris-Lyon service. *Brian Perren*

Above right:
This picture shows the summit of the line at Col du Bois (north of Mâcon). The track is *in situ* and mast erection is in progress. On the right side of the picture is the formation of a new road which runs parallel with the railway for a short distance. *SNCF/Delemarre*

Right:
Two TGV units coupled together are seen at speed north of St Florentin. *SNCF/CAV*

TGV

Above:
The construction of Lyon Part-Dieu station was part of a major reorganisation of railway facilities in the Lyon area.
SNCF/Broncard

Lyon reorganisation

Creation of the LGV necessitated a major reorganisation of the flow of traffic through the Lyon area, but the alterations at Lyon were far more complex than those in Paris. The Lyon reorganisation was necessary for a number of reasons. As the only suitable point of entry to Lyon for the LGV was at Sathonay, this effectively limited the future role of Perrache as Lyon's major SNCF station. Traffic forecasts for TGV assumed a substantial increase in business, necessitating a significant increase in the number of trains to be worked through the Lyon area. As well as an hourly service of TGVs to/from Paris, a number of trains bound for the Rhône Valley, Marseille and Montpellier were henceforth to pass through Lyon without stopping.

Thus, even if Perrache had been more accessible to the LGV route, there was insufficient capacity to cope with the new levels of traffic and no prospects for expansion. At the north end of the station all traffic including freight had to be worked through the 2,108m two-track St Irénée Tunnel. The south of the station area itself is located between bridges which carry the railway over the River Saône at the north end and the River Rhône at the south.

Fortunately, the tracks from the LGV junction at Sathonay passed through the old Brotteaux station and an adjoining large piece of land at Part-Dieu which the SNCF had been using for a small freight terminal. Like Perrache, Brotteaux station was unsuitable for further development, but Part-Dieu offered the space and potential

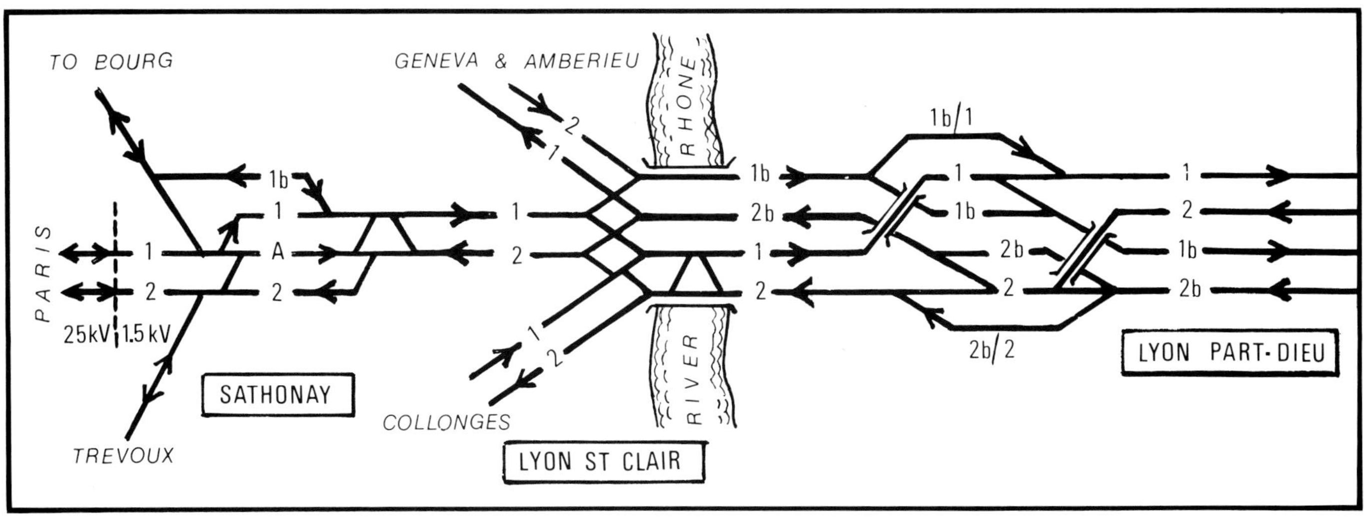

Below:
To pass trains to/from the LGV at Sathonay a series of junctions and flyovers were built between Lyon St Clair and Part-Dieu.

SNCF was seeking. An agreement was made between SNCF and the Lyon urban authority to promote a joint venture, with outside financial participation, to develop the Part-Dieu site as a combined station, business and shopping complex. Part-Dieu has good access for private cars, buses, taxis and the Lyon metro. Ticket sales, reservations, restaurant facilities and shops are located in a spacious shopping area. Access to the four platform lines is by escalator, stairs and a ramp and there is a lift for handicapped passengers. The station is now one of the most modern in Europe.

Under the reorganisation, Part-Dieu became the primary interchange station for long-distance passengers and Perrache was retained as a terminal point and local interchange. During the past few years extensive improvements have also been made to Perrache which is well equipped with new facilities including an excellent taxi, bus and metro interchange. With the start of the full TGV service in September 1983, the final phase of the traffic reorganisation was implemented. The new routeings are:

(1) TGVs off the LGV terminating at Lyon enter the area at Sathonay and call first at Part-Dieu. From Part-Dieu they continue to Perrache where they complete their journey. TGVs between Paris, St-Etienne or Grenoble — which often run in multiple with a unit for Lyon Perrache — divide/combine at Part-Dieu from whence they continue independently to Guillotiere where they follow their respective routes.

(2) TGVs off the LGV bound for the Rhône Valley and Marseille/Montpellier — most of which do not stop at Lyon — pass through Part-Dieu and join the Rhône Valley line at Guillotière.

(3) Locomotive-hauled trains from North-East France to the south and southwest which use the PLM route through Dijon and Mâcon were rerouted between Collonges-Fontaines and St Clair to Part-Dieu instead of Perrache, resuming their main route to the Rhône Valley at Guillotière. Cross-

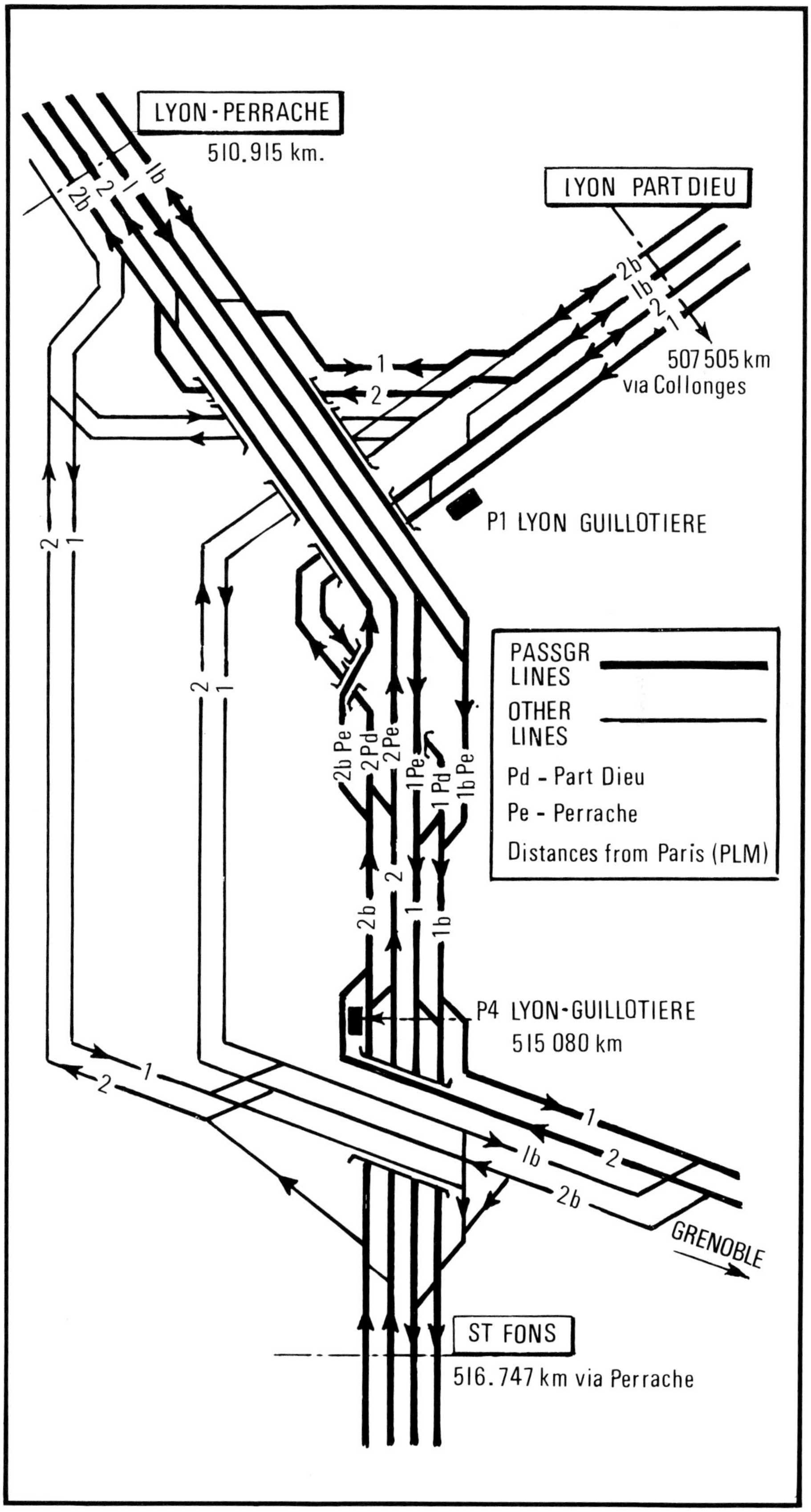

Above:
A diagram illustrating the principal junctions in the Lyon area.

Table 2: La Ligne a Grande Vitesse (LGV): exact distances

	Cumulative distance from Paris (km)	*Cumulative distance from Paris (miles)*
Paris (Gare de Lyon)	—	—
Start of LGV: Lieusaint	29.4	18.27
Le Creusot TGV station (273.8km from Leiusaint)	303.2	188.41
Mâcon-Loché TGV station (334.0km from Lieusaint)	363.4	225.82
End of LGV: Sathonay (389.3km from Lieusaint)	418.7	260.18
Lyon Part-Dieu	427.2	265.46
Pasilly Junction (161.8km from Lieusaint)	191.2	118.81
End of LGV: (177.0km from Lieusaint)	206.4	128.25
Dijon-Ville	284.7	176.91
Savoy Junction (337.7km from Lieusaint)	367.1	228.12
End of LGV: Pont de Veyle (344.2km from Lieusaint)	373.6	232.16
Bourg-en-Bresse	402.9	250.36
Geneva	549.2	341.27
Chambéry	521.9	324.31
Valance (106.8km from Lyon Part-Dieu)	534.0	331.83
Avignon (124.4km from Valence)	658.4	409.13
Montpellier (98.5km from Avignon)	756.9	470.34
Marseille (120.3km from Avignon)	778.7	483.88

Because of variation in the length and location of some platforms and junction layouts, there are some minor variations in some distances.

country services from Nantes also terminating at Lyon Perrache also use the route via St Clair and Part-Dieu before terminating at Perrache.

(4) No change was necessary to the cross-country, regional and international trains from Strasbourg, the French Alps and Turin via Modane.

(5) The foregoing changes released capacity for freight trains coming through Lyon via the PLM line to Perrache and then by the loop through Oullins before taking their route to the south. This was an important element in the SNCF's freight train working strategy. With this opening of the LGV, they were able to segregate daytime passenger and freight trains over the 550 or so miles between Paris and Marseille. Freight trains now use the PLM line through to Lyon, the Oullins loop and the right bank of the River Rhône, while passenger trains use the LGV and the Rhône Valley right bank. It must be emphasised that this strategy was an important part of the economic case for the LGV project.

Mention should finally be made of the new work undertaken in the Lyon area to cope with this traffic reorganisation. To cope with the considerable increase in train movements between St Clair, the new Part-Dieu station and Guillotière, additional tracks were installed controlled by a new signalbox at Part-Dieu. To eliminate conflicting train movements at St Clair, flyovers have been provided enabling parallel movements to and from Collonges, the LGV and the Geneva line. To facilitate the passage of trains from Part-Dieu to Perrache and to the Rhône Valley main line, a series of flyovers were built in the Guillotière area to eliminate a number of flat junctions. With through train services concentrated on the bypass line via Oullins, the junction layout at Givors has been simplified to eliminate conflicting movements.

Below:
A two-unit Lyon-Paris service passes through the old Lyon Brotteaux station which was replaced by Part-Dieu in June 1983. *Brian Perren*

3.

Paris-Sud Est A Market-Led Success

Marketing the PSE

Everybody in France knows about the TGV, even if they have not yet used it themselves. It may be a cliché, but the French really do love their railways. The technical success of the Paris-Sud Est (PSE) railway generated a sense of national pride as well as new business for both TGV and other routes with conventional trains. However, national pride *per se* does not sell seats on trains and the growth in business owes much to the efforts and skills of SNCF's marketing people. But first some impressive statistics. From 1982-85 the number of passengers using the TGV rose from just under six million to 14.7 million. Taking 1982 — the first full calendar year of TGV services — as a reference point (equals 100), passengers using the new services rose to 150 by the end of 1983, 223 by the end of 1984 and 247 by the end of 1985. As the Lausanne service did not start until 22 January 1984, 1985 was the first full calendar year of TGV services on that route.

The two major business successes of TGV-PSE are Lyon and Geneva. To a large extent the tremendous growth in rail business between the French capital and the country's next most important city was predictable. With the Paris journey time halved to just 2hr, an hourly service spread from 06.00 to 21.00 with extra trains during the peak periods, SNCF's proven reliability and fares pitched at a level where they are not a major item in average disposable income, a good measure of success was to be expected. Nonetheless, the rate of growth has exceeded the expectations of even the most optimistic members of SNCF management. So far as the business market is concerned, TGV has more or less defeated its principal competitor Air Inter (the French domestic airline) which previously enjoyed the lion's share of the market. By the end of 1984 some 1.2 million passengers — equal to 56.5% of the market — had transferred from air to TGV. Even allowing for the poor location of Lyon's Satalos Airport — which is about 12 miles to the east of the city — there is no way that the city-to-city time by air can be less than 3hr. TGV is also more frequent and its fares are lower.

Table 3: TGV Paris (Gare-de-Lyon)-Lyon (Part-Dieu) Standard running times

	km (1)	*Cumulative* (2) *point-to-point time:mins*	*Theoretical* (3) *section times*
Paris Gare-de-Lyon	—	0	
Lieusaint Junction	29.4	15	15.00
PRS10 Moissy	2.1	15+	0.50
PRS11 Le Châtelet	25.9	22	6.50
PRS12 Marolles	49.2	27+	5.65
PRS13 Cuy	71.4	33	5.45
PRS14 Vaumort	92.7	38+	5.20
PRS15 Verigny	117.0	44+	6.00
PRS16 Tonnerre	139.8	50	5.45
PRS17 Pasilly Junction	162.1	55+	5.55
PRS18 Toutry	182.0	60+	5.00
PRS19 Lacour D'Arcenay	202.3	65+	5.30
PRS20 Vianges	225.8	71+	5.90
PRS21 Sully	207.4	76+	5.20
PRS22 Montchenin	273.7	83	6.40
PRS23 Vaux-En-Pré	292.9	88	4.70
PRS24 Cluny	315.5	92	4.90
PRS25 Mâcon Loché	333.9	97	5.00
Junction to Savoy	337.7	98+	1.00
PRS27 Cesseins	341.1	104+	5.80
PK 386.4	386.4	112+	8.00
Sathonay station	389.3	113+	1.00
St Clair Junction	—	117+	3.80
Flyover	—	118	2.70
Lyon (Part-Dieu)	8.5	120	120.00
Total: Paris-Lyon	427.2		

PRS: signal relay post
PK: km post

(1) Cumulative distances — Gare-de-Lyon-Lieusaint Junction; Lieusaint-Lyon Part-Dieu.
(2) Timetable times (+shows a gain over theoretical times).
(3) Theoretical times calculated by computer.

Following an in-depth analysis and appraisal of the first five years' results, SNCF has concluded that the Lyon-Paris market could be sustained by three simple basic criteria: journey time, frequency and price. (Reliability is so good, that it is not normally an issue.) This by itself is apparently sufficient to generate a 5% annual growth. When visiting other countries one is tempted to look at their markets in a British context. For example, would peripheral stops in the outer suburbs of Paris or Lyon attract more customers, and is

Table 4: Passengers Using TGV Services 1982-85: Rate of Growth

Year	*Lyon St Etienne (incl Lille-Lyon) (×1,000)*	*(%)*	*Dijon Franche-Compté Lausanne (×1,000)*	*(%)*	*Geneva-Savoie (Annecy; Chambéry etc) (×1,000)*	*(%)*	*Rhône Valley Marseille Mediterranean (×1,000)*	*(%)*	*Total (×1,000)*	*(%)*	*Notes*
1982	3,726.9	100	383.5	100	688.4	100	1,172.8	100	5,971.6	100	(1), (2), (3)
1983	4,025.3	108	665.1	173	1,399.2	203	2,872.7	244	8,962.3	150	(4), (5)
1984	4,818.9	129	2,301.8	600	2,409.7	350	3,794.6	324	13,325.0	223	(6)
1985	5,317.7	143	2,534.1	660	2,693.2	391	4,189.0	357	14,734.0	247	

(1) Public service commenced in 1981 over southern section of route to Lyon, Dijon, Besançon and Geneva.
(2) Additional services introduced in May 1982 to Rhône Valley, Montpellier and Marseille.
(3) Services to Rhône Valley, Montpellier and Marseille increased in frequency from September 1982.
(4) Services to Chambéry and Annecy introduced in May 1983.
(5) Full TGV service (except to Lausanne) introduced 25 September 1983.
(6) Paris-Lausanne service introduced 22 January 1984; launch completed.

there scope for a Pullman or 'Nouvelle Première' type of on-board service between Lyon and Paris? The answers were very interesting.

As the two main residential areas in Lyon are located within easy access of Perrache and Part-Dieu and as the TGV route does not pass through a suitable suburban railhead such as Watford, this was not a practical option. However, a large number of local stations — particularly those in residential areas — are equipped as TGV sales points where a passenger can go to buy a ticket and make a reservation. At the Paris end, on the other hand, the situation is quite different. Analysis of passengers using TGV services at Paris showed that many

had travelled considerable distances before joining the TGV at the Gare de Lyon. From these figures SNCF concluded that if TGV was causing a spin-off as far north as Lille to the extent that passengers were prepared to cross Paris, the market would probably support a direct Lille-Lyon TGV, which would eliminate the change of terminal station in Paris. In September 1984 a new service departing at 07.13 from Lille to Lyon calling at Douai, Arras and Longueau (Amiens) was launched with a return northbound service in the evening. About 750 passengers per day were soon using the service and from May 1986 a second complementary pair of trains, north from Lyon in the morning and south in the evening, was introduced.

Experience with the Lille-Lyon service has led to a second marketing initiative aimed at the western part of the outer Paris suburban area where there is an existing market of passengers using early morning TGVs from the Gare de Lyon. To meet and expand this existing market a new service was launched in September 1987 leaving Rouen for Lyon at 08.00, with stops at Nantes-la-Jolie and Versailles, and arriving at Lyon at 11.50; there is a northbound return service in the evening. Connections to and from Caen are provided at Nantes-la-Jolie.

SNCF do not see any reason to lift the on-board service on the Paris-Lyon TGVs up market with a 'Nouvelle Premiere' or similar market concept. 'Nouvelle Premiere' was a response to a specific market situation where air competition was eroding the market base for First Class travel, but was not commercially viable. As this is not the case on the Paris-Lyon route and the extra cost of the service would not generate additional net revenue, this concept cannot be justified for business travel. As previously stated, the emphasis is on journey time, frequency and price. However, this does not imply that on-board service is not regarded as important. Train meals, served airline style, are available to First Class passengers at their seats and cost Fr39 (£3.90) for a continental breakfast and Fr140 (£14.00) for lunch or dinner. The quality of the four-course lunch and dinner trays has been considerably improved and they are now good value for money.

The combined importance of journey time and frequency shows in the timetables. A journey time of 2hr between Paris and Lyon opens up excellent journey opportunities for such a distance. Except on Mondays, when there is an 05.15 from Part-Dieu to Paris, the first service is at 05.50, giving a Paris arrival at 08.06. This is followed by trains at 06.30, 07.00, 07.06 and 08.00 — giving a total of four (five on Monday)

Below left:
A new direct TGV service between Lille and Lyon was introduced in 1984 and was subsequently increased to two workings per day in each direction. Unit No 53 arrives at Lille with the 09.42 from Lyon. *David Haydock*

Below:
A train conductor checks the reservations of passengers who have just boarded a TGV. *SNCF*

Bottom:
Lunch service in First Class. *SNCF/CAV*

Above:
The original design of TGV bar. The present cramped layout is to be expanded when units pass through main works for overhaul. *SNCF/CAV*

Left:
SNCF's mid-1970s comprehensive marketing revamp covered passenger access and reception as well as on board amenities. Customer care — emphasised by the word *acceuil* for service — is the theme of the passenger business. New uniforms have been introduced for train conductors. *SNCF*

Right:
In Lyon a completely new station, financed by a joint venture with outside companies, was built at Part-Dieu to cope with the extra business generated by TGV. *Top right:* **The main hall;** *Right:* **the concourse and departure indicator;** *Far right:* **various passenger facilities;** *Below right:* **the ticket selling points with a special window for handicapped passengers** *Far right:* **the departure platforms.** *SNCF*

arrivals in Paris by 09.10. Similarly, three early services out of Paris will get you to Lyon by 09.00 followed by two others arriving at 09.30 and 10.02. Early business trains also run to and from Grenoble and St Etienne as part of the basic Lyon service. The last services are at 21.10 from Lyon to Paris and 21.00 from Paris to Lyon, but with a later service to Lyon at 21.50 on Fridays and Sundays. The small fleet of nine all-First Class units are used to cope with the business peaks. For example, an all-First Class unit forms the 05.48 from Grenoble as far as Part-Dieu, where it couples to a two-class unit from St Etienne. Another First Class set is used in the 09.00 from Part-Dieu to Paris. Similarly, the 07.30 from Paris to Lyon is all-First Class. The all-First Class units are also used for evening peak business trains.

For the greater part of the day — ie between the business travel peaks — loadings on the Paris-Lyon TGV are largely dependent on optional passengers. Off-peak travel is actively promoted. No supplements are imposed and only basic fares are charged. Here again, journey times and frequency have been the main selling points. A very large proportion of the growth in Second Class journeys is from 'creative' traffic. With greatly reduced journey times it is now possible to undertake journeys for pleasure or social purposes over distances which were hitherto impossible.

Geneva: rail business revitalised

If the success of TGV between Paris and Lyon was to some extent expected, this was not the case between Paris and Geneva. Before the start of the first stage of TGV operations, rail did not have a very large slice of this market. So far as the business traveller was concerned air had — and looked like retaining — the largest share. The airlines priced accordingly. Their fares were high and seating capacity rarely matched potential custom, to the extent that it was often difficult to book a seat other than well in advance. This gave them very good load factors. Prior to the advent of the TGV the physical nature of the route made it impossible for rail to compete in terms of journey times. Almost all rail passengers between Geneva and Paris travelled by way of Lausanne, Vallorbe and Dijon. Two good trains were provided. The 'Jean-Jacques Rousseau' provided a through Geneva-Paris and the 'Cisalpin'. TEE offered a good connection from Geneva via a quick change at Lausanne. The second route between Geneva and Paris ran from the Savoy Alps via Bellegarde, Culoz, Bourg-en-Bresse and Mâcon, thence over the old PLM main line. This route was never a serious contender for Paris traffic. Between Geneva and Culoz the line, some of which is single track, follows a steeply- graded, tortuous route through the Alps. Consequently, journey times were slow. To serve various towns in the Savoy Alps, such as Chambéry, St Gervais, Evian and Annecy, and to cater for Italian traffic through Modane, SNCF operated multi-portion day and night services to and from Paris. Geneva was served by a daytime two-coach portion from Paris which was included in one of these trains, but the time to Paris was much slower than the already uncompetitive journey times by way of Lausanne.

The advent of TGV changed this situation. Detailed analysis of the Geneva-Paris situation convinced SNCF that the TGV would give them the means to make a re-entry into this very promising market. The constraints of the Alpine line would be more than offset by the tremendous saving of time on the new railway between Mâcon and Paris. To gain business from the airlines, SNCF had to get as close as possible to a 3hr centre-to-centre time. Notional timings showed that a schedule of about 3½hr was perfectly possible. Having regard to the nature of the route this is very fast. The difficult nature of the section of route through the Alps is indicated by the TGV's operating schedule. Paris to Pont-de-Veyle (where Geneva trains leave the high speed line) is booked to take 100min with 110min less to cover the section from there on to Geneva. Thus, 48% of the journey time is used for 68% of the distance, leaving 52% of the time for the final 32% of the journey through the Alps. Even so, the average journey speed between Paris and Geneva is 157km/hr (97.7mph). Even though a 3½hr TGV service was marginally slower than the journey by air, SNCF felt confident that they would be successful. Standard fares were cheaper than by air, the railway would be adding seating capacity to an under-sold market, it had all-weather reliability and TGV — which offered more passenger space and better general ambience than an aircraft — was after all Europe's latest and fastest train. There was bound to be a 'sparks' effect.

At first only two trains per day were provided but, even before the whole TGV route was fully operational, a third was soon necessary. With the start of the full service in September 1983 a fourth service was added. By June 1986, with traffic still rising, a fifth train was added to the service. By the end of 1984, 233,000 passengers per year who had previously travelled by air between Paris and Geneva had transferred to TGV — a transfer of 32%. Geneva TGVs were carrying about 1,500 passengers per day compared with 470 by air. Now, with five trains each way, TGV offers a total of 1,930 seats per day in each direction.

4.

Paris-Sud Est Operations

TGV timetables and workings

Five years have now passed since the first section of the new railway was opened but, apart from a few changes and extensions to meet the market, the basic concept, whereby each group of services has been designed to carry the maximum number of passengers between Paris and the main centres of population with the minimum number of intermediate stops, has been retained. Because the population of

Table 5: TGV (PSE) Journey Times

Journey	*Distance (km)*	*Time (hr min)*	*Speeds (km/hr)*	*(mph)*
Paris-Mâcon Loché	363.4	1.40	218	135.5
Lyon Part-Dieu-Paris	427.9	2.00	214	133.0
Paris-Lyon Part-Dieu	427.2	2.00	213.6	132.7
Paris-Le Creusot	303.2	1.25½	212.8	132.2
Paris-Bourg-en-Bresse	402.9	1.57	206.6	128.39
Paris-Montbard	213.4	1.05½	195.5	121.5
Paris-Valence	534.0	2.54	184.1	114.4
Paris-Dijon	284.7	1.36	177.9	110.5
Culoz-Paris	483.6	2.44	176.9	110.0
Paris-Avignon	658.4	3.45	175.6	109.1
Paris-Bellegarde	515.8	2.59	172.9	107.4
Longeau-Lyon Part-Dieu	563.8	3.21	168.3	104.6
Paris-Geneva	549.2	3.23	162.3	100.9
Paris-Aix-les-Bains	505.2	2.55	173.2	107.6

Below:
TGVs are coupled or uncoupled at Lyon Part-Dieu. With its coupling compartment open, this unit is leaving Lyon Perrache for the short journey to Part-Dieu where it will join another unit which started its journey at St Etienne. After coupling at Part-Dieu the two units will go on to Paris.
Brian Perren

Above:
A two-unit TGV leaves Avignon on a non-stop run to Paris. *Brian Perren*

Below:
TGV has greatly improved communications between Paris and the Savoy Alps region. This Geneva-Paris TGV is calling at Bellegarde to take up passengers from Evian; it then runs forward non-stop to Paris. *Brian Perren*

France is thinly spread over a large geographical area, the distances between the principal towns and cities are often considerable. On the old PLM line, for example, there are only four centres of any importance — Dijon, Lyon, Valence and Avignon — in the 863km (536 miles) of route between Paris and Marseille. There are only two intermediate stations — Le Creusot and Mâcon — on the LGV. For the same reasons — although there are a number of important cross country routes — the French national system radiates outwards from Paris. Given the foregoing, SNCF is often able to run some of its principal trains over considerable distances without the need for an intermediate stop. Paris to Bordeaux — 581km (361 miles) — was the best example, but now some TGVs run non-stop between Paris and Avignon — a distance of 658km (409 miles). The PSE train services divide into four groups: Paris-Lyon/Grenoble/St Etienne; Paris-Rhône Valley-Montpellier/Marseille; Paris-Geneva/Savoy Alps and Paris-Dijon-Lausanne.

As discussed earlier the Paris-Lyon service carries the biggest of the PSE traffic flows and is sufficient to support a regular-interval timetable. This is a new development for SNCF, for while their suburban services have always been organised on this basis, traffic volumes on main line routes have hitherto been insufficient to support either an hourly or even a two-hourly regular pattern. At first the only extension of the Lyon service was the portion working of three TGV units to give a through service to the industrial town of St Etienne, which is 54km (34 miles) to the southwest of Lyon. Grenoble is also served as part of the Lyon service, but this facility was not introduced until March 1985 when the route from Lyon to Chambéry and Grenoble by way of St André-le-Gaz was electrified. Before the commencement of TGV operations

Above:
EuroCity interchange at Lausanne. The daytime service between Milan and Paris via the Simplon is now provided by Swiss or Italian trains which cover the section from Milan to Lausanne where passengers change to the TGV. *Swiss Railways*

Grenoble, which is an important centre with a population of 160,000, was served by diesel-hauled 'Corail' trains to and from Paris or local DMUs. The impact of TGV on the Grenoble market — the journey time to Paris is now around 3¼hr — was just sufficient to justify the case of extending electrification from Lyon. There are six services in each direction between Paris and Grenoble. TGV originating from or terminating at Lyon start or finish their journey at Perrache station. They all stop at Part-Dieu where trains with Grenoble or St Etienne units combine or divide. With automatic couplers this operation is very quick and efficient, but a couple of extra minutes are required to position or clear the leading unit. Although 2hr for the non-stop run between Part-Dieu and Paris (Gare de Lyon) is the usual time quoted for this journey, some trains are allowed an extra 2 or 4min for pathing reasons to ensure punctual running. However, unless the train ahead is late most drivers adhere to the 2hr schedule.

While SNCF has retained the basic TGV timetable structure on the PSE network, the operating department has always been ready to support their marketing colleagues when ideas for new or extended services have been proposed. The first of what I am sure will be a continuing trend of new marketing initiatives was the Lyon-Lille through TGV service which was mentioned in the earlier section on PSE marketing. To provide the Lille service it is necessary to take a TGV unit well away from its normal area of operation, but this was relatively easy to organise. As the PSE fleet is cleared for universal operational availability throughout the SNCF electrified areas, only the provision of train crews and overnight maintenance at Lille had to be arranged. In line with SNCF operating policy it was decided to run the Lille service non-stop from its second stop at Lyon Part-Dieu to the first passenger stop at Longeau (Amiens) which is 126km (78 miles) out of Paris (Nord) on the Nord region main line to Lille; this is a distance of 564km (350 miles) from Lyon Part-Dieu. From Lyon to Lille the service runs the length of the new line to the big Paris railway centre at Villeneuve-St Georges (11km or 7 miles from Gare de Lyon) where it diverted on to the Grande Ceinture route. The Grande Ceinture is a series of lines which forms a complete circle around Paris providing access for the transfer of traffic through the capital. It is electrified throughout (partly at 1,500V dc and partly at 25kV ac) and is mostly used by through freight services such as those running from the Port of Marseille into northern areas such as Lille. It is also used by a number of important overnight international services.

The time allowed for the 564km (350 miles) from Lyon Part-Dieu to Longeau is 3hr 21min — an average speed of 168.3km/hr (104.6mph). This astonishing schedule is accomplished despite the tortuous 30min passage of the Grande Ceinture where the maximum speed is never higher than about 100km/hr (62mph) and within the maximum line speed of 160km/hr (100mph) on the Nord main line.

With the addition of a second Lille TGV to the service from the start of the 1986 summer timetable, this operation is now performed by two trains per day (seven days per week) in each direction. From the start of the winter service on 28 September 1986, the running of one pair of trains has been modified to accommodate the new service between Rouen and Lyon which was mentioned earlier.

Paris-Rhône Valley-Montpellier/Marseille

Before the advent of TGV, the service between Paris, the Rhône Valley, Montpellier and Marseille was provided by locomotive-hauled trains calling at

Right:
Villeneuve St Georges TGV maintenance depot. Equipment in this workshop can lift a complete eight-car articulated unit from its bogies. *SNCF/CAV*

Dijon, Lyon-Perrache, Valence and Avignon. A number of these trains ran beyond Marseille to serve the coastal resorts of the Côte d'Azure through to Nice. With the introduction of TGV the Rhône Valley trains were established as a separate service which passed through Lyon without stopping. However, to maintain a service to the principal stations on the old PLM route, a revised pattern of locomotive-hauled 'Corail' services has been retained. One of these trains still runs all the way from Paris to Nice by this route, but the other services all start or terminate at Metz in North East France.

When the TGV-PSE network was being planned, SNCF looked at all target schedules with a critical commercial eye to see how or if TGV journey times compared with the competition. In principle, of course, all services running beyond Lyon would offer a 2hr reduction over their previous journey times, but was it possible to exploit the superior acceleration and braking characteristics of the TGV over conventional track with standard signalling? An obvious case for study was the 218 miles of route south of Lyon through the Rhône Valley to Marseille. The Rhône Valley line does not have the potential to be developed as a high-speed route. Although parts are suitable for speeds of 200km/hr (125mph), some sections of the route suffer from severe curvature which imposes a number of permanent speed restrictions.

However, an evaluation of the Rhône Valley route showed that four zones totalling 96km (60 miles) could be upgraded from 160 to 200km/hr (100 to 125mph) at reasonable cost. Given potential savings of about 10min for each TGV service the budget was prepared and a programme of works involving track, structures, level crossings, power supplies and signalling was implemented during 1984. Given the basic potential of the LGV plus the Rhône Valley upgrading, train services between Paris and Valence, Avignon and Marseille/Montpellier have been drastically improved. Now TGVs from Paris run at least as far as Valence (534km or 332 miles) without a stop, but some run non-stop between Paris and Avignon (658km or 409 miles). The Paris-Avignon non-stops, which are scheduled to complete the journey in 3hr 45min at an average speed of 175.6km/hr (109mph), represent the peak of contemporary SNCF operating achievement. The best journey time between Paris and Marseille is now 4hr 40min.

With the reduction of journey times over the Rhône Valley route, SNCF decided to use a pair of Paris-Marseille TGVs to provide a fast morning and evening business service in each direction between Lyon and Marseille. Hitherto, all Rhône Valley TGVs passed through Lyon without stopping and this market was served by locomotive-hauled 'Corail' trains. It is now possible to travel between Lyon and Marseille in just over 2hr 40min.

A controversial feature of the new service was a decision by the SNCF not to run the TGV beyond Marseille which would be the terminus for all services from Paris. Daytime passengers from Paris to Toulon, Cannes, Nice and the Italian border station at Ventimiglia would have to change trains at Nice. Connections between Marseille and Nice were maintained by a service of locomotive-hauled trains. As mentioned earlier a through 'Corail' service between Paris and Nice was also retained. New passageways and escalators were installed at Marseille St Charles to facilitate passenger interchange.

SNCF defended their decision on several grounds. The TGV was not really suitable for a journey of about 7hr and there were insufficient units to cover the 2½hr extension from Marseille to Nice. Needless to say this decision provoked widespread expressions of dissatisfaction by passengers who were strongly supported by the local authorities along this important part of the French Mediterranean coast. As this part of France is primarily a holiday area, passengers on these trains normally travel with a considerable volume of luggage. Humping this baggage across Marseille station by passengers who have hitherto enjoyed the through service was also a considerable source of irritation to the extent that SNCF decided to extend two TGVs as far as Toulon. This is 67km (42 miles) from Marseille and did much to alleviate the problem. But dissatisfaction from Cannes and Nice passengers still persisted. To some extent passenger growth between Paris and the Côte d'Azure stations was not as good as on other TGV routes. However, SNCF's fears that the PSE sets would not be suitable for long journeys has not been supported by market research — passengers like the TGV as a symbol of modern rail travel. From the beginning of April 1987 a daily TGV between Paris and Nice was introduced with a journey time of 7hr. This is supplemented by a First Class Paris-Nice service on Saturdays and a return Nice-Paris service on Sundays.

Paris-Geneva/Savoy Alps

TGVs for the group of destinations in the Savoy Alps — Geneva, Annecy and Chambéry — come off the LGV at Pont de Veyle shortly after passing through Mâcon. From Pont de Veyle they use the old PLM line through Bourg-En-Bresse as far as Ambérieu where they join the Lyon to Geneva line. Between Pont de Veyle and Ambérieu the line speed is 160km/hr (100mph), but then as the line enters the mountain area the route follows a tortuous course and the line speed is reduced. At Culoz the route to Geneva and Chambéry part company. Geneva trains run down the valley — of which 17km (11 miles) is inside Swiss territory — to complete their journey at the SBB station. Incidentally, at Geneva the railway is operated as a single entity with SNCF trains stabled in the Swiss sidings, but the two platforms used by French services are segregated for customs and passport purposes.

From Culoz the main route turns south passing Aix-les-Bains, which is the junction for the Annecy line, before reaching Chambéry. Trains from Paris bound for Annecy have to reverse at Aix-les-Bains. The distance from Culoz to Chambéry is only 36km (22 miles).

With the exception of Geneva — an international city of considerable business and political importance — which now has a service of five TGVs each way to and from Paris, it has always been difficult to serve the Savoy Alps region. Both Annecy and Chambéry are sufficiently important to justify through trains to Paris, but the same train cannot serve both places. Also, there are feeder services from other important centres in the French Alps —Evian, St Gervais and Bourg-St-Maurice — which have to connect with the TGV services to and from Paris.

At first SNCF decided to serve this region with two TGV units as far as Culoz where they would divide for Geneva or either Annecy of Chambéry. Also, some Annecy and Chambéry services run as a two-unit formation as far as Aix-les-Bains. However, as business increased, particularly to Geneva, traffic built up to a point where separate independent TGVs could be justified for most destinations. At weekends and during the summer and winter holiday peaks, it is often necessary to run two-unit formations to each destination to cope with the traffic.

Below:
A Paris-Lyon TGV awaiting departure.
A. Taylor

Below right:
A two-unit service at full line speed.
SNCF/Fabbro

Paris-Dijon-Lausanne

Of all the TGV services running from Paris through Dijon, that for Besançon and Lausanne in Switzerland is probably the most complicated. When this group of services, which came off the high-speed line at Aisy whence they use the old PLM route as far as Dijon, was planned, the major complication was the international traffic between Paris and Lausanne in Switzerland and Milan in Italy, previously conveyed by locomotive-hauled trains over the Swiss border at Vallorbe. All that was necessary at Vallorbe was a brief stop to change locomotives and carry out passport and customs checks. Vallorbe is a small town whose only importance is its role as a border station. From the outset the SNCF and the SBB saw that the only practical way of handling this traffic was to run the TGV into Switzerland, at least as far as Lausanne. Lausanne, which generates a good level of passengers for Paris, is a natural break point in the working. Accordingly, SNCF agreed to equip a small number of TGVs (the total is now eight) for working under the Swiss catenary where power supplies are taken at 1,500kV 16⅔Hz. They are also equipped with the Swiss 'Integra' cab signalling aid.

Less easy to resolve was the problem of the through traffic from Paris to the Simplon stations and Milan. The possibility of a through TGV to Milan was a non-starter on grounds of cost and practicability. At least three extra TGV sets would be necessary and the whole 'Swiss' sub-fleet would have to be equipped to take power supplies at 3,000V dc when running in Italy, as well as the single Swiss and two French systems.

Given these constraints it was clear that passengers travelling to points beyond Lausanne would have to change trains. The SNCF, SBB and FS (Italian Railways) recognised the commercial disadvantage of imposing a change of train on customers who had hitherto enjoyed a through service. However, a service has been organised to make the change of train as painless as possible. The service is arranged so that three out of the four Lausanne-Paris TGVs in each direction make a cross-platform connection with a SBB EuroCity train which starts from or terminates at Geneva. So as to emphasise the through nature of the service the SBB trains all carry the same name 'Lutetia', 'Cisalpin', 'Lemano' — as the TGV with which they connect.

As well as making connections for Milan the Lausanne TGVs also provide a service to the Swiss capital city Bern by means of a Swiss service connecting with the TGV at Frasne. The Swiss feeder service was provided by one of their TEE RAe EMUs. However, from the start of the summer service in June 1987, a separate TGV is provided between Paris and Bern. The Bern unit will be attached to the evening service from Paris and the morning service from Lausanne; it will be attached to/detached from the main Lausanne unit at Frasne. Following the success at Geneva, SBB are very anxious to use the proven appeal of the TGV to develop business between Paris, Bern and possibly Interlaken.

Introduction of the Lausanne TGV service, which did not start until January 1984 when all the 'Swiss' three-voltage units had been delivered, cut journey times by about 1hr. As is the case with the Savoy Alps services, once off the new railway the TGVs have to cope with a line speed of 160km/hr (100mph) for the greater part of the route between Aisy and Dole, but once into the Jura mountain area progress is much slower because of permanent speed restrictions. Journey times between Paris and Lausanne are about 3hr 50min. I should mention that part of the saving has been made by streamlining border formalities, thereby eliminating the need for a long station stop which was a feature in the past.

The basic Lausanne service of four trains in each direction is also used as a basis for SNCF's own domestic service to Dijon, Besançon and Chalon-sur-Saône. All of the Lausanne TGVs work as a two-unit service either to Dole, where a unit for Besançon is split off,

or as far as Dijon. There are also other independent services between Paris, Dijon and Besançon. Sufficient business was on offer for SNCF to provide two services beyond Dijon over the PLM route to Chalon serving Beaune in each direction.

In order to keep the small sub-fleet of 'Swiss' three-voltage units in this part of the network, they are programmed to cover most of the foregoing services, but at peak periods some of the two-voltage units may be used for services to Dijon, Besançon and Chalon-sur-Saône, but not of course to Lausanne. Some workings call for a three- and a two-voltage unit to work in multiple.

Day-to-day 24hr supervision of all TGV operations — train running, monitoring of loadings, modifications to schedules, and the maintenance of track, power, and signalling — is masterminded from a central operations post near Gare de Lyon in Paris. Briefly summarised, the function of this space-age centre is to ensure that the trains run to time, that customer demand is met by providing extra capacity where necessary and that maximum revenue earning potential is achieved by ensuring good load factors on each train. There are four separate activities, and all the controllers working in the centre are located together for easy contact.

Traffic and energy control

This section is responsible for traffic control, which is achieved by means of permanent radio links with the drivers on the trains, supported by computer-based information systems, for resolving any operational difficulties which may arise and for taking such steps as may be necessary to minimise disruption to the service. They also control and monitor the supply of power from the sub-stations to the catenary.

Operations control

Essentially the job of the operations control group is to supervise the work and disposition of the TGV fleet. While the workings of the individual units are arranged in advance by the timetable production department in the normal way, unforeseen circumstances often make it necessary to modify a unit working at very short notice. For example, a small defect may detain a unit in the depot beyond the scheduled maintenance time and another train has to be positioned to take its place. Late running, or a unit failure on the road, will also make it necessary to adjust rosters and position another replacement train. Operational control is carried out by close and constant contact with the two main Paris installations — Bercy Conflans Depot and Villeneuve workshops — together with the 14 or so locations in the Provinces (plus Geneva and Lausanne) where TGV units are parked overnight.

However, an interesting feature of TGV is the flexibility built into the system whereby units and crew can be organised at short notice to provide a relief service. Known peak traffic days — Fridays throughout the year, holiday peaks and public holidays — can be provided for in advance, but special events may generate additional traffic. Operation Control's job involves the monitoring of the computer seat reservation system to see if a particular service is booking heavily at specific times in advance. At a given loading ratio it may be decided to strengthen the train from a single to a two-unit formation or provide a complete duplicate service. Provision of the extra unit may involve a positioning trip on a scheduled service to a provincial centre or an arrangement to work the additional unit back to Paris as soon as possible. Train crews and catering also have to be organised. If a single-unit service becomes a two-unit service, an additional catering crew is of course also necessary.

Below:
During the construction of the Sud Est railway, great care was taken to preserve the environment; many bridges and viaducts were built for the new line.
SNCF/Delemarre

Programme control

This section compiles schedules for track maintenance work which is carried out during the day or night and monitors these activities in liaison with the appropriate engineering departments.

The despatching and signalling centre (PAR)

In British terms the PAR centre combines the role of a signalling and traffic control centre. PAR's control area coincides with the new railway and its outer limits at Lieusaint, Aisy, Pont de Veyle and Santhonay. Trains are passed to or received off the new line by contact between the PAR centre and the neighbouring conventional signalboxes. PAR operates by means of four computerised, electronics-based systems for the monitoring of signalling installations and traction current supply, the track diagrams and control panels for signalling and energy supplies together with the operator's control desk and corresponding circuits, a computerised train describer and route control systems and a central hot axlebox detection system. This hot axlebox detection system operates by means of an infra-red detector device which gives the temperature of the axleboxes and records various measurements each time a train passes. Data is stored and then transmitted to the control centre which if necessary will bring the train to a stand or warn the driver that he should run at the reduced speed.

The traffic controller, who is in charge of both despatching and signalling, sits in front of an impressive track console which gives him a general view of the pattern of all TGV traffic and the conditions existing at any given moment. From a semi-circular balcony overlooking the despatching centre it is possible to survey the installations as a whole without disturbing any of the staff at work.

Table 6: TGV (PSE) Fleet Composition:

Unit Type	*Seats*	*Number of Units*	*Unit Nos*
First Class, two-voltage	285	9	33-38, 100-102
First/Second Class, two-voltage	First: 111 Second: 275 Total: 386	92	01-32, 39-98
First/Second Class, three-voltage	First: 111 Second: 275	8	110-117
	Total Passenger Units:	109	
TGV Postal		2	PO1, PO2

Fleet utilisation

All 109 passenger TGV sets — plus the two postal units — are allocated to the Paris-Sud Est servicing depot at Bercy Conflans just outside the Gare de Lyon. At Bercy Conflans units are cleaned and receive basic maintenance at given intervals in the rosters based on a combination of time and distance. Heavy maintenance — including the lifting of the eight articulated cars off their bogies — is undertaken at a new purpose-built workshop at Villeneuve St Georges known as AMPSE (Atelier Matériel Paris Sud Est). Five separate sets of unit diagrams are prepared to cover what SNCF call 'basic days' which are Tuesday to Thursday (which count as one), Friday, Saturday, Sunday and Monday. Table 7 sets out the disposition of the fleet by the three types of unit for each of the five programme days. The table also shows the overnight stabling points and the number of units reserved for unprogrammed strengthening or relief work which may be organised on an ad hoc basis — often only a day or so in advance. The unit workings are organised on a circuit basis so as to achieve equal mileage accumulation for each individual unit. Incidentally, there are no spare trailer cars in the TGV passenger fleet and thus if there is a defect the entire 2+8 set is taken out of service.

Because of the importance of the weekend peaks, as much non-routine work as possible is carried out either at night or on Tuesdays, Wednesdays, or Thursdays. During the summer timetable (the details shown are based on the summer of 1986) the weekend load tends to carry over from Friday through to Sunday and a total of 76 two-class two-voltage sets are required, but this includes 10 extra sets for strengthening or relief purposes. Similarly, seven two-class three-voltage 'Swiss' sets are used, but only one set is in reserve on Saturday. If there is need for a relief for a two-unit service to Lausanne during the weekend this would have to be covered from the 'Swiss' sub-fleet. In these circumstances one or two of the three-voltage sets would be taken off a Dijon or Besancon service and replaced by a standard two-voltage set. Until the introduction of the new First Class-only section in service between

Table 7: TGV stabling points for booked workings winter 1986-87:

Stabling Point	*Two-voltage First/Second Class*					*Two-voltage First Class*					*Three-voltage First/Second Class*				
	M	*Tue Thu*	*Fri*	*Sat*	*Sun*	*M*	*Tue Thu*	*Fri*	*Sat*	*Sun*	*M*	*Tue Thu*	*Fri*	*Sat*	*Sun*
Paris Bercy-Conflans	38	28	36	24	31	3	2	2	(2)	(2)	2	3	5	3	4
Lyon Scaronne	6	7	7	13	9	2	3	3	(3)	(3)					
Grenoble	1	1	1	2	2	1	1	1	(1)	(1)					
St Etienne	1	1	1	1	1										
Valence	1	1	1												
Lille	1	1	1	1	1										
Montpellier	4	5	6	6	6										
Marseille St Charles	4	4	4	6	6										
Toulon	2	2	2	3	3										
Besançon	2	1	1	2	2										
Lausanne											2	1	1	2	1
Chalons-sur-Saône	1	1	1	1											1
Geneva	2	2	2	3	2										
Annecy	1	1	1	2	3										
Chambéry	2	2	2	2											
Booked Workings	66	57	66	66	66	6	6	6	(6)	(6)	4	4	6	5	6
For relief/strengthening	—	5	10	10	10	—	—	1	7	7	1	1	—	1	—
Fleet Operational Total	66	62	76	76	76	6	6	7	7	7	5	5	6	6	6

Paris and Nice, none of the First Class sets normally worked on Saturdays or Sundays and this posed the familiar problem of the utilisation of specialised stock. While they are definitely required for Monday to Friday peak work they are under-utilised at most other times. To remedy this situation, SNCF is looking at the possibility of altering the seating configuration so that the layout comprises four First and three Second Class coaches (plus the buffet) instead of seven Firsts (plus the buffet) which will enable the fleet to be used at the weekend.

Table 8 sets out the seven-day extract from the two-voltage unit cyclic working which is a typical example of how the units are programmed. Over a seven-day period the unit will cover 14 services accumulating a total of 8,973km (5,576 miles). Note the extended layover period at Paris (Note 1) on Monday, Wednesday and Thursday allowing ample time to cover any necessary maintenance. Table 9 sets out the total and average kms programmed for each operational day.

Table 8: Seven-day Roster for Two-voltage TGV unit First/Second Class

Day	*Terminal*	*Arr*	*Dep*	*km*	*miles*	*Notes*
1 Mon	Toulon	—	11.26			
	Paris	16.50	—	848	527	(1) 15hr
2 Tue	Paris	—	10.34			
	Geneva	14.03	16.50			
	Paris	20.31	—	1,102	685	
3 Wed	Paris	—	07.35			
	Geneva	11.08	12.57			
	Paris	16.32	—	1,102	685	(1) 12hr
4 Thur	Paris	—	07.24			
	Annecy	11.00	12.02			
	Paris	15.44	16.43			
	Chambéry	20.02	—	1,609	1,000	(1) 12hr
5 Fri	Chambéry	—	10.40			
	Paris	13.57	18.33			
	Montpellier	23.22	—	1,280	795	
6 Sat	Montpellier	—	08.04			
	Paris	12.49	17.47			
	Montpellier	22.37	—	1,518	943	
7 Sun	Montpellier	—	08.45			
	Paris	13.47	15.40			
	Montpellier	20.25		1,514	941	
				8,973	5,576	

(1) Extended times for maintenance at Bercy-Conflans Depot (Paris)

Table 9: Daily Programmed kms winter 1986-87

Day	*Monday*		*Tuesday-Thursday*		*Friday*		*Saturday*		*Sunday*	
	Total	*Average*	*Total*	*Average*	*Total*	*Average*	*Total*	*Average*	*Total*	*Average*
Two-voltage, First/Second Class	72,613	1,320	71,396	1,298	84,927	1,286	64,351	1,170	74,340	1,161
Two-voltage, First Class	8,043	1,340	8,073	1,345	6,769	1,128	—	—	—	—
Three-voltage, First/Second Class	5,054	1,263	4,406	1,101	7,294	1,215	5,979	1,195	6,943	1,157
Total kms	85,710	—	83,875	—	98,990	—	70,330	—	81,283	—
Total miles	53,260		52,120		61,512		43,703		50,509	

5. The Atlantique Project

Within SNCF the Atlantique project (TGV-A) started to crystallise in 1975 as a follow on from TGV-PSE, but public discussion did not begin until the autumn of 1981. When President Mitterand inaugurated the first (southern) section of TGV-PSE on 22 September 1981, he asked SNCF to prepare plans for TGV-Atlantique. Early in 1982 the SNCF Board of Directors had approved the project and sent a report to the French Government summarising the technical details and describing the principal economic features. The Ministry of Transport then set up a study group, who undertook a detailed critical examination of the project. Their favourable response was received on 1 July 1982. Finally, a Cabinet meeting in November 1983 gave its approval to the 'Public Utility' process. As a 'Declaration of Public Utility' gives wide powers to a state concern — including the compulsory purchase of land — the consultation procedure is very thorough. TGV-A was declared a 'Public Utility' on 25 May 1984.

Given the state of French economy at that time, and cutbacks in public spending, one would have thought that a major state project such as TGV-A would have been deferred, but funds were made available. That work started immediately, showed a Government commitment to national infrastructure — in particular railways — far greater than other countries in Europe and possibly the world. However, by the middle of 1984 the brilliant technical and commercial success of TGV-PSE was already apparent.

A good case for TGV-A

As with TGV-PSE, the economic case for TGV-A is not based on the provision of high-speed services *per se*, but is an integrated project to increase capacity to cope with future levels of both passenger and freight business. The basis of the project is: the existence of a substantial demand on the trunk routes from Paris (Montparnasse) to the west and from Paris (Austerlitz) to the southwest; saturation of the present lines and their inability to cope with foreseen levels of both long-distance and regional traffic; and the desirability of having a new line with a modern terminal in the Paris region.

In 1980 rail traffic on the west and southwest trunk routes was 15.5 million

Below:
An illustration of the anticipated investment required for the civil engineering structures involved in the construction of the TGV Atlantique project. The estimates are as foreseen in June 1980 and exclude VAT.

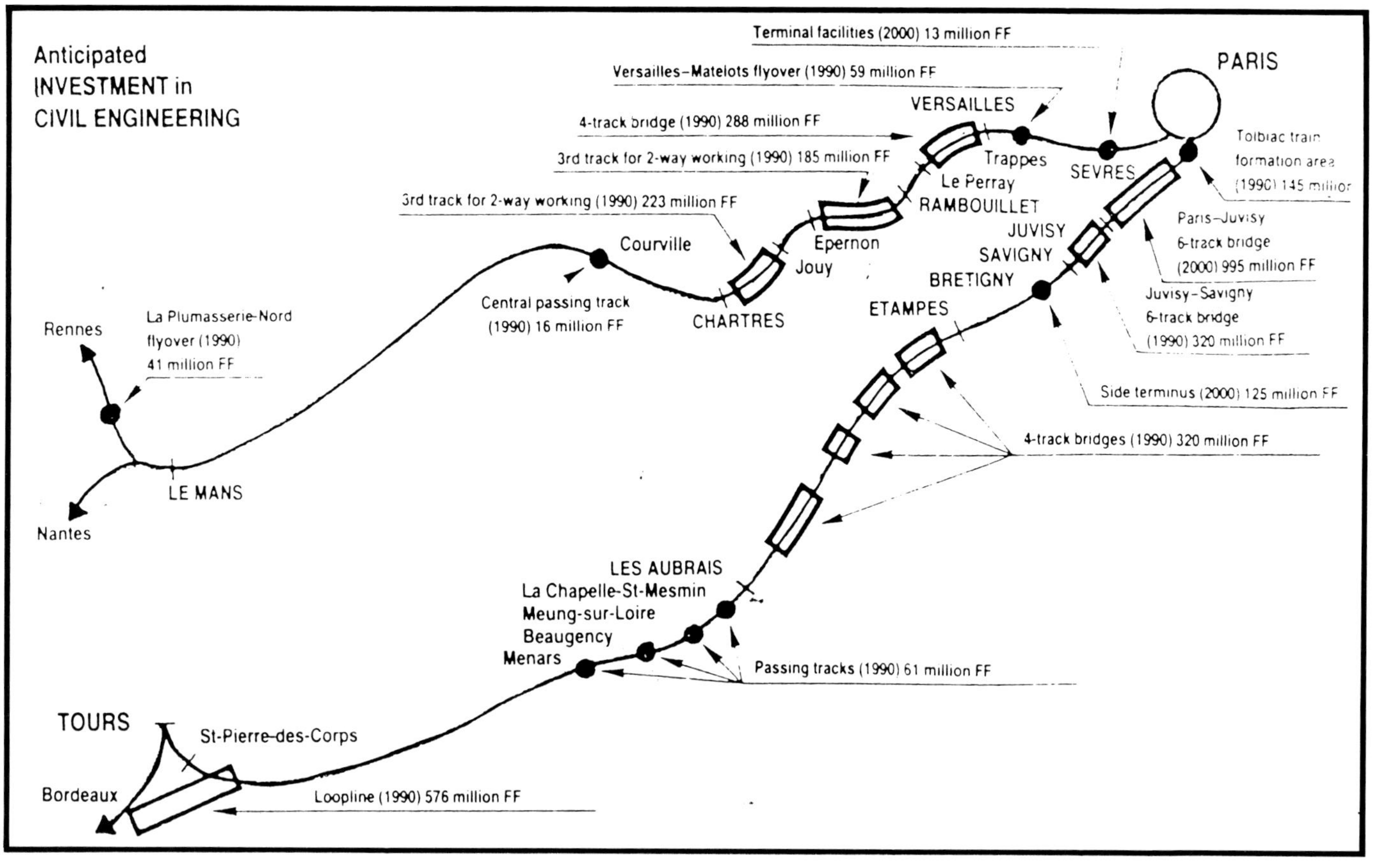

journeys, divided almost equally between the two routes. In journey-number terms this traffic is greater than the Paris-Sud Est route before the building of TGV-PSE. Assuming a modest growth in the French economy, an increase in consumer spending, small population growth, an improvement in conventional rail services without TGV, lower air fares and increased motorway construction, by 1990 rail journeys should reach 18.8 million. This is an increase of 18% from 1980 to 1990, but without the now confirmed passenger appeal of TGV.

As well as the long-distance business on the existing Paris-Le Mans and Paris-Tours lines, other substantial flows of traffic have to be moved. They include: Paris inner and outer-suburban traffic, fast and semi-fast trains for the Loire Valley and stations between Chartres and Le Mans, and national and international freight trains. Timetabling of traffic with varying speeds and braking characteristics poses a number of problems, particularly at pressure points in the Paris area, the Loire Valley and the approaches to Le Mans and Tours. Other complications include the overlapping of the commuter and inter-city peaks out of Paris in the late afternoon, the need to integrate both west and southwest suburban services with Regional Express (RER) line C, and the convergence of cross-country routes at Le Mans and Tours.

However, elimination of the long-term capacity constraints could be achieved with a programme of infrastructure improvements. The cost of these works (at 1980 prices) amounted to a staggering total of Fr825 million for the Le Mans and Fr2,542 million for the Tours route. At the current rate of exchange — but excluding inflation — the total is of the order of £320 million. Moreover, this enormous financial cost — plus the environmental disturbance — would only solve the problems of the suburban and outer Paris areas. Signalling, track geometry and track spacing preclude raising the line speed above 200km/hr. The quality of the main line services in terms of frequency and speed would remain unchanged and the long-term business prospects for express services to these regions would be much less favourable with little gain in market share.

280km (174 miles) of new railway

In view of the foregoing, SNCF looked at the alternative costs of a TGV route which would carry the combined west and southwest passenger services from the centre of Paris to rejoin the existing network beyond the present traffic bottlenecks. Studies confirmed that, by using the infrastructure of the old abandoned Gallardon line from Paris (Montparnasse) to Chartres — which was completed with single line to

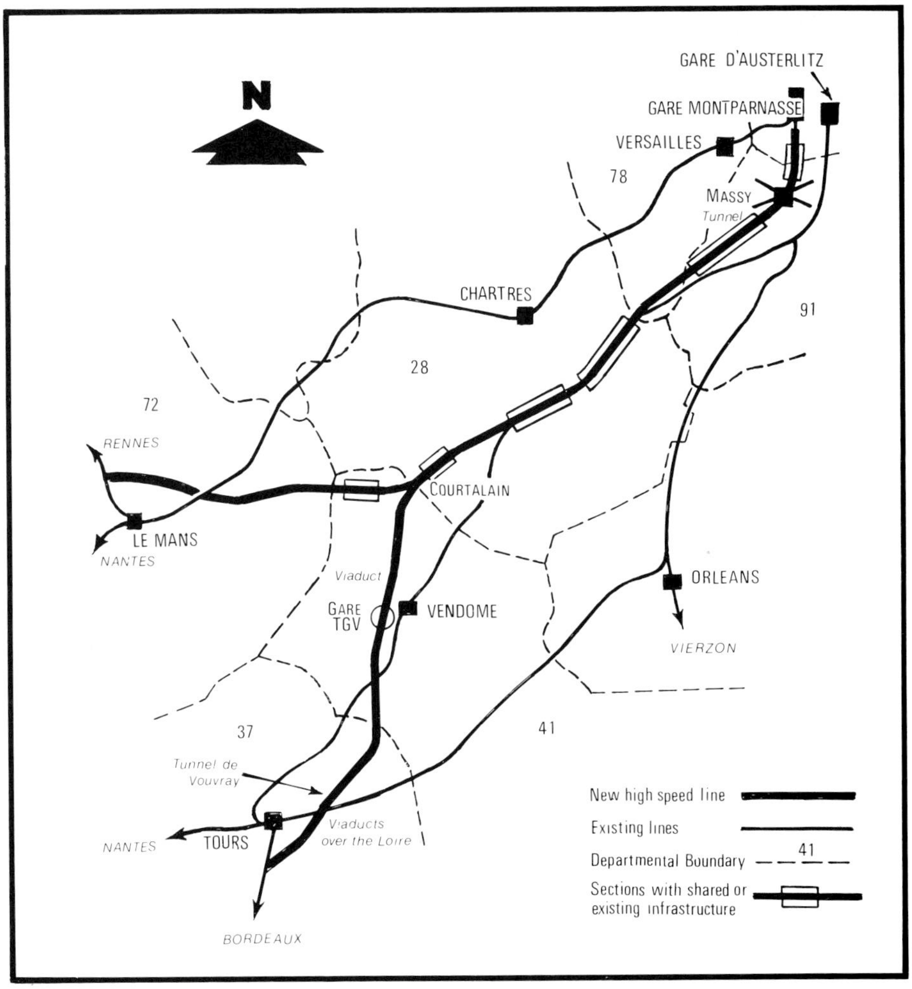

Above left:
Work is well in hand on the new TGV-Atlantique project which — unlike its PSE predecessor — will run into the heart of Paris terminating a couple of miles from Paris Montparnasse terminal. This has been made possible by using the old Gallardon line. This aerial picture shows the course of the new TGV route; Paris skyline is in the background. *SNCF*

Above:
TGV-Atlantique. Work in progress on Fontenay Tunnel in the outer suburbs of Paris. When complete the tunnel will be covered over to minimise environmental disturbance. *SNCF/CAV*

Left:
The projected route of the TGV-Atlantique.

Massy-Palaiseau in the Paris suburbs in 1914 but eventually abandoned in 1938 — SNCF planners had a potential route from the centre of Paris to the west/southwest. The new railway starts at Malakoff, just 3km from the existing layout at Montparnasse. Totalling 280km (174 miles) the TGV-A project is Y-shaped and comprises 124km (77 miles) from Bagneux to the junction at Courtalain; 52km (32 miles) from Courtalain to Connerré where it joins the Paris (Montparnasse)-Chartres-Le Mans line almost 23km (14 miles) east of Le Mans; 87km (54 miles) from Courtalain to St Pierre-des-Corps (Tours) on the Paris (Austerlitz)-Bordeaux main line and a final 17km (11 miles) for the Tours loop. (When the Paris [Austerlitz]-Bordeaux line was built it bypassed both Orléans and Tours. Terminal stations were however built at both towns, but almost without exception Paris-Bordeaux trains use the through avoiding lines to obviate reversal. A stop is made at Les Aubrais for Orléans and St Pierre-des-Corps for Tours, from where EMU shuttle trains make connections.)

Route characteristics and superstructure

Compared with TGV-PSE, which was built with a maximum gradient of 35%, TGV-A gradients will not exceed 15% except at seven locations where the gradient will be 25%. The highest point of the line is 200m. However, whereas TGV-PSE has no tunnels on its route, TGV-A has 2,600m of double-track and 9,600m of single-track tunnels at Villejust. Following tests these tunnels have been built to a wider gauge to overcome aerodynamic problems. In single-bore tunnels the free space (ie the air section) is 45sq m and can be used at 200km/hr (125mph) and 72sq m in larger single-bore, double-track tunnels which can be used at 270km/hr (168mph).

As is the case with all new major SNCF electrification projects, power supplies will be 25kV ac for the new line, but with the exception of the Tours loop which will be 1,500V dc. The new trains — which will be dual-voltage 25kV ac/1,500V dc — can thus work throughout the network. There are significant sections of both 1,500V dc and 25kV ac on the SNCF Western lines, but most of the South Western lines — including 816km (507 miles) trunk route from Paris (Austerlitz) through Bordeaux to the Spanish Frontier at Hendaye — is 1,500V dc. Cab signalling similar to that in use on TGV-PSE will be installed throughout the new railway.

Paris (Montparnasse) remodelling

To cope with the high increase in train movements, the volume of passengers using the new TGV-A services and also to provide facilities for in-and-out working at certain platforms, Paris (Montparnasse) station is to be comprehensively remodelled. This work will include the entire terminal layout and complex of crossovers, sidings, yards, and stabling points located in the 6km as far as Châtillon. The present layout at Montparnasse dates from 1964 when the old station was closed and — under 'Operation Maine-Montparnasse' — completely rebuilt. This project was financed partly by a joint venture with private companies, funded by the construction of the huge but controversial Montparnasse Tower, which today still dominates the Paris skyline.

To cope with the increase in business new points of access for passengers arriving both on foot and by taxi will be built. A separate concourse for suburban passengers and a new TGV departure hall will be provided. A new station entrance, with staircases to the passenger platforms, will be built from the Cinq Martyrs Bridge. The new platforms will be designed to take a raft above the whole platform area. The possibility is being studied of building a two-storey structure, with 50,000sq m of office space on the lower level and recreation facilities on the upper.

As the new TGV-A tracks start/terminate within 3km of Montparnasse station, a new flyover carrying one of the TGV tracks over most of the other roads so as to provide access to the arrival group of platforms is to be built. The flyover will also be used for empty TGV sets returning to the new TGV Depot and by trains leaving for the Versailles direction. All tracks will be bi-directionally operated.

Montrouge Depot, currently the base for 750-800 locomotive-hauled vehicles used for the main line services from Montparnasse to the West of France, is to be adapted as the base for the new TGV-A fleet of trains. Here there will be facilities for pit inspections, interior and exterior cleaning, the emptying of chemical toilets and the checking of sandboxes and pantographs. When completed the new depot will eventually comprise five 500m tracks for servicing short turnround sets, six other tracks for cleaning, inspection and emptying toilets, a building housing eight 250m tracks with inspection pits, two machines to wash trains on the move and 500m of track for stabling and despatch.

Second generation TGV

The contract for the construction of the new fleet of 95 train sets for the Atlantique project was signed on 18 November 1985, the first units being scheduled for delivery in 1988. After acceptance trials the new trains will be used for crew training, technical and commercial evaluation trials and the replacement of locomotive-hauled services from Paris to West and South-West France. The tender procedure for the Atlantique fleet was initiated in September 1984; the build was again awarded to Alsthom who are the leaders of a construction group developed with Francorail. Thus, Alsthom's very successful collaboration with SNCF from the start of the PSE project has been maintained.

While the Atlantique fleet will outwardly resemble their PSE predecessors, the new trains are in every

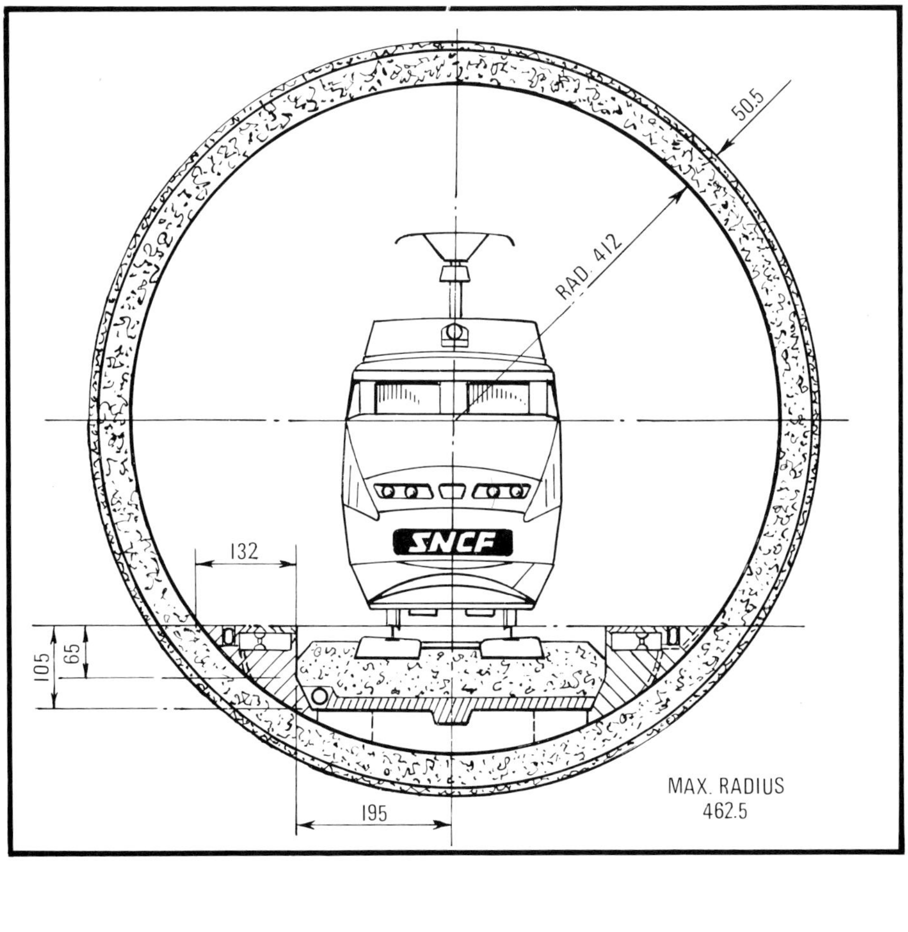

Above:
An artist's impression of the proposed TGV-Atlantique train. *SNCF/Vignal*

Below left:
Unlike the PSE line which has no tunnels, the Atlantique line will have a number of tunnels including 9,600m of single bores at Villejust. To permit speeds of 200km/hr the tunnel has been bored to a larger than normal profile.

respect 'second generation' TGVs. The development of a new series of technical specifications follows the experience gained with the PSE fleet — the design of which is now over 10 years old — which has enabled SNCF to identify specific areas for improvement. These are passenger comfort, performance and cost. However, while the design team has been encouraged to seek a significant degree of progress, they have resisted the temptation to multiply the number of new technical innovations. To keep the cost of the Atlantique fleet within closely defined parameters but also to allow certain technical developments to be pursued, each new specification has been costed so that it can be considered on its own merits.

Compared with the PSE trains, the major differences for the 'Atlantique' trains are formation, speed and traction. The new trains will have 10 instead of eight trailer vehicles. As with the PSE fleet, the 10 trailers will be in a fixed articulated unit marshalled between the two power cars. The maximum speed of the sets will be 300km/hr (186mph). The increase in weight and speed is partly due to the easier gradients on the Atlantique line, but the major factor is the development of the synchronous traction motor. These new motors can each produce 1,100kW (1,475hp) instead of 535kW (717hp) by the motors in the PSE sets, but with equivalent bulk and lower volume. The synchronous motors can also produce 1,300kW (1,742hp) when accelerating away from a standing start. It is also possible to make a standing start on a 25% gradient with one motor isolated and the train operating on only 75% of its maximum power.

Thus, sufficient power will be produced for the extra weight and increased maximum speed with only four motor bogies per train instead of six in the PSE sets. To accommodate six motor bogies on the PSE sets, one motor bogie is located at the outer end of the leading and trailing end of the eight-car articulated vehicle unit. On the Atlantique trains all motor bogies — two on each vehicle — are under the two power cars. The maximum speed of the Atlantique trains on conventional parts of the SNCF system will also be raised from 200 to 220km/hr in either dc or ac mode. (The 200km/hr section between Le Mans and Nantes is electrified at 25kV ac, whereas the 200km/hr sections on the Bordeaux route are supplied at 1,500V dc.)

To cope with these higher speeds, the braking system has been redesigned with the use of high-powered, non-ventilated disc brakes in combination with an anti-skid device controlled by micro-processors. Because it allows speeds of 300km/hr (186mph) with a lighter bogie, noise levels and maintenance costs are both reduced. The use of non-ventilated discs also consumes less energy.

To ensure efficient current collection at 300km/hr, a new pantograph has been designed with a unique large plunger with a second stage which has also been redesigned. The new ac pantograph — known as the GPU — has considerably improved aerodynamics which reduces its sensitivity to side winds. The new GPU design will also be adapted for the train's dc pantographs to cope with current collection at speeds up to 220km/hr (137mph) with all four pantographs raised when two units are working in multiple. The southwest catenary — installed many years ago when train speeds were

Right:
The new railway takes shape at Chatillon-en-Dunoys 120km from Paris Montparnasse. *Alan Sprod*

Left:
First Class 'Club' seating. *SNCF/Olivain*

Centre left:
First Class ordinary seating. *SNCF/Vignal*

Bottom left:
A First Class saloon for group accommodation located in an end vehicle. *SNCF/Fabbro*

around 120km/hr (75mph) — will also have to be modified for collection at higher speeds. Some additional feeder stations will also have to be provided.

To ensure a good ride at the higher speeds, the suspension for the Atlantique trains has been completely redesigned. Following a programme of practical tests with PSE Unit No 10, a new system of pneumatic suspension — combining comfort and economy — has been developed. A new bogie — the Y237 — has also been designed and will supersede the Y231 which was used on the PSE sets.

Outwardly, with the exception of the reshaped profile on the higher point of the two power cars which has achieved a more integrated roof line, the Atlantique trains look similar to the PSE sets, but the livery has been changed. To emphasise the fact that the new trains are 'second generation', the brilliant red-orange finish used on the PSE trains will be replaced by a new finish in silver-white and blue with red parts on the upper sections of the doors. As well as providing a more comfortable and efficient train, the new technical innovations will save energy. The current consumption costs of each set will be reduced by Fr200,000 (£20,000) per year — almost £2 million for the whole fleet.

Enhanced passenger environment

As I mentioned earlier, the original design and layout of the PSE accommodation is simple and functional. When it was designed 10 or so years ago it was thought to be perfectly adequate for the 2hr Paris-Lyon journey where the bulk of the business would be drawn. In fact, in response to market growth, PSE trains are now used on much longer journeys such as Lille/Rouen-Lyon and Paris-Nice. However, given SNCF's market-led profile and determination to generate the maximum amount of business from all market sectors through well-researched initiatives, the facilities in the Atlantique trains have been completely revamped.

The First Class accommodation will have a completely new design concept incorporating some of the ideas from 'Nouvelle Première'. Each of the three First Class trailers in each set will offer a different choice of seating layout. All will be suitable for the provision of meal service at seats from a small aircraft-type galley.

In line with current commercial policy, the new trains will reflect SNCF's

Above:
A Second Class saloon with children's play area. *SNCF/Vignal*

intention to make the service even more attractive for family journeys and young people travelling Second Class. In general there will be an increase in face-to-face seating. In two adjacent vehicles, small areas ('Espace Enfants') for families with young children will be formed from four bays of four seats each with a nursery and toilet. This space will be provided by folding seats which provide room for children to play. At the end of each set, a compartment of 16 lifting seats will be specially provided.

The criticism of the small and cramped buffet bar in the PSE sets has been well taken. SNCF has dedicated a whole vehicle for a redesigned catering/lounge area in the Atlantique sets. Located between the groups of First and Second Class coaches, a totally different style of décor will emphasise its aspect as a place to linger. It will comprise three areas: a shop, where a variety of goods will be on sale; the central part with shelf-tables and bar stools; and finally the bar area with tables and tip-up seats. In addition, public telephones will be installed. A redesigned, more effective air conditioning system will also be installed throughout the train.

Train services

TGV-A will replace the present service of conventional locomotive-hauled daytime trains from Paris (Austerlitz) to Tours, Poitiers, La Rochelle, Bordeaux, Tarbes and the Spanish border at Hendaye. They will run to/from Paris (Montparnasse) over the new high-speed line as far as St Pierre-des-Corps or the end of the new Tours loop. From St Pierre-des-Corps, TGVs will run over the existing Bordeaux line which will be upgraded from 200 to 220km/hr (125 to 137mph). Trains currently running from Montparnasse to Le Mans, Nantes, St Nazaire and destinations in Brittany will use the new railway to Connerré, and then continue on existing tracks. Except for the section from Le Mans to Nantes — which will also be upgraded from 200 to 220km/hr, 160km/hr (100mph) will be the ruling speed to other places west of Le Mans. These higher speeds will entail modifications to both the catenary and signalling.

A problem exists for Bordeaux line passengers in that overnight trains will continue to run to/from Austerlitz station in Paris, with the use of different terminals for day and night services. This will have an effect on the provision of peak services to South West France. If anticipated business on late evening PSE services exceeds TGV set availability, it is generally possible to run an extra locomotive-hauled service from the Gare-de-Lyon to cater for these passengers. As a locomotive-hauled relief for South West France will have to run from Austerlitz station, while passengers will be congregating at Montparnasse looking for seats on TGVs, a relief service from a neighbouring terminus involving a bus, taxi or a metro journey is hardly practical. Thus the SNCF has set the size of the TGV-A fleet and the enlarged capacity at Montparnasse station, to meet peak requirements.

Draft timetables for TGV-A have been planned on the basis of an hourly service from Paris to Rennes, Nantes and Bordeaux, except at slack periods, but with more frequent stops. There will be 14 return journeys to/from Rennes and Nantes and 15 to/from Bordeaux. Together with other destinations the mid-week service will total over 50 TGVs in each direction, divided more or less equally between the West and South West branches. Dramatic cuts in journey times will be made. The distance by the new TGV-A route to St Pierre-des-Corps is about 6km longer than the present route through Orléans and is almost exactly the same to Le Mans compared with the route via Chartres. Le Mans gets the fastest journey time of 1hr at an average speed of 211km/hr (131mph). Since the existing route between Paris (Montpar-

Left:
Second Class seating. *SNCF/Henri*

nasse) and Le Mans has a number of locations where speed has to be reduced below 160km/h, TGV-A gives a particularly good improvement to Le Mans. Bordeaux time is cut from 4hr 4min to 2hr 58min raising the present best average speed from 143 to 198km/hr (89 to 123mph). The best average speed from Paris to Le Mans is lifted from 131 to 211km/hr (81 to 131mph). This best average of 211km/hr to Le Mans falls slightly below the best TGV-PSE 2hr time from Paris to Lyon Part-Dieu at 214km/hr (133mph). Since the distance to Lyon is double that to Le Mans, the opportunity for sustained high speed is greater and consequently produces a higher average.

Although the times shown for journeys to stations west of Rennes to Brest and Quimper and from Poitiers to La Rochelle, assume that these routes will be electrified, the only project currently in progress is over the 101km from Rennes to St Brieue. Completion of the other routes, which have yet to be authorised, will not be ready for the completion of TGV-A. Passengers will have to change trains.

There will be two new stations on the Atlantique line:

Massy-Palaiseau

Located 14km from Montparnasse terminus, Massy-Palaiseau will be an important TGV railhead covering the west of Paris and nearby Versailles (population 95,000). The station, which will be below ground level in a cut-and-cover section, will have a connection with the existing station served by RER lines B and C. A large car park will be provided.

Vendôme

Passengers from the Loire Valley town of Vendôme (population 18,200) will have a new station with a direct service to/from Paris in 49min. The present service between Paris and the existing station at Vendôme (178km from Paris) is provided by a DMU from Paris (Austerlitz) as far as Dourdon and then over a branch line and takes about 2½hr.

Cross-country possibilities

A criticism of SNCF services concerns the long cross-country journey times between important provincial centres — such as from Nantes to Lyon, from Bordeaux to Lyon, or from Lyon to Strasbourg — compared with the high speed of services to or from Paris. Apart from the provision of new 'Corail' stock, it is very difficult to improve French cross-country services. Many of the routes have diesel haulage, gradients and track geometry preclude decent speeds and the low level of traffic necessitates frequent intermediate stops. Such is the speed of TGV, that many cross-country journey times could be improved even if this entails a longer distance by way of Paris. The Lille-Lyon through TGV, which bypasses Paris, is a great success and has been increased to two services each way. A route with good passenger potential, both for business and leisure travel, is that from Nantes to Lyon, but the present journey time is about 7hr for the 650km (404 miles) — a distance equivalent to that from Euston to Glasgow. But by using TGV-A, the Paris 'Grande Ceinture' route and TGV-PSE it will be possible to run from Nantes to Lyon in about 4hr. SNCF see this as a good commercial prospect and with TGV-A there will be at least one service each way from Nantes with the possibility of a second service from Rennes to Lyon. During the holiday periods — including both the summer and winter peaks — trains could go beyond Lyon to Chambéry or the Rhône Valley. With their lower power-to-weight ratio, TGV-A sets would not normally be used on the steeper PSE line, but a small number of the TGV-A sets will be modified for interconnection services. Trains will leave the TGV-A at Massy-Palaiseau and using the RER lines will proceed to Vallenton where they will reverse to gain access to the South East.

Investment and timing

The total cost of the railway (excluding the trains) is about £687.6m (see p31). The first stage of the project will be the common part of the route to Courtalain and the West branch to Le Mans. This will open for public service in the summer of 1989. Work on the South West branch did not start until the first half of 1986 and will open for the public in October 1990. The state is to contribute 30% to the total cost of the project; the rate of profitability will be 10% for SNCF and 20% for the whole enterprise. Some 20 million passengers per year could be carried by TGV-A from the first year of service — an increase of 33% on the routes concerned. From 1990 when the entire project is finished it will complete, together with TGV-PSE, a high-speed railway network serving 75% of the French population, and will generate 40% of SNCF's total passenger traffic.

Below left:
A more spacious bar and on board shopping area.

6.

Towards a European Network

If various projects currently in hand or under study bear fruit, Europe could have a network of high-speed routes heralding the start of a new railway age by the year 2000. Key to the European dimension is TGV-Nord and the Channel Tunnel which will form the core of a basic network extending from Paris to London, Brussels, Amsterdam and Cologne. If West Germany proceeds with a plan to build a TGV-type high-speed corridor from Cologne to Frankfurt, high-speed services could run into the heart of the German Federal Republic. Although Paris is seen as the terminal for most TGV-Nord services, the prospects for through trains to other parts of France are so strong that SNCF has plans to build a series of new connections in the Paris area which would link TGV-Nord with the PSE and Atlantique lines as well as the proposed TGV-Est route to Strasbourg. By this time TGV-PSE will have been extended from Lyon to Marseille anyway. The various projects are examined in detail below.

Below:
Map illustrating the projected European TGV network.

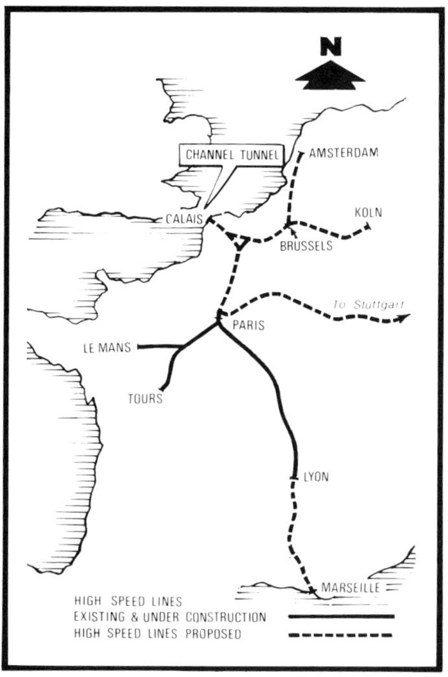

TGV-Nord

In July 1983 a working group comprising the Transport Ministers of France, Belgium and West Germany produced a study into the possibility of a high-speed railway linking Paris, Brussels and Cologne. A year later, in July 1984, this working group, which also included representatives of the national railway administrations, was given the go-ahead to develop their preliminary findings into a more detailed plan. Also, their mandate was extended to include the possibility of a branch into the Netherlands terminating at Amsterdam. All aspects of the project have been studied, but the legal and financial areas are seen to be particularly difficult. The budgetary and legal procedures of each country have to be respected, but each country's consultation and legal processes differ to a considerable extent. Only an agreement on a Government-to-Government basis would be sufficient to give the project the necessary momentum. While the joint French, Belgian, Dutch and West German study group was working on the project, a new and somewhat unexpected development began to take shape: the possibility of a 'fixed link' between Britain and France.

The idea of a channel tunnel is now very old and work has already started on two occasions only to be subsequently abandoned. In 1971 a protocol was signed between the British and French Governments and a private group, but preliminary work was terminated in 1975. But surprisingly in September 1981, the issue was reopened when a working group of five British and French banks concluded that a permanent link between the two countries would be financially viable. In November 1984 the two Governments confirmed their determination to facilitate the building of a fixed link, but with the important proviso that the project would exclude Government financing or guarantees.

Given the chequered history of the Channel Tunnel concept, both the British and French Governments have given their support with an unusual degree of determination and urgency. A very tight timetable was set. In April 1985 tenders were invited for submission by 31 October 1985 with the final outcome to be made by the end of January 1986. At a ceremony in Lille on 20 January 1986, the British Prime Minister, Margaret Thatcher, and President Mitterand of France announced that the two Governments had given approval to the project promoted by the Channel Tunnel Group to build a 7.3m diameter twin-bore rail tunnel. The Channel Tunnel Group's rail-only solution had been won on technical, commercial and environmental grounds. It was the best researched and detailed plan. The Tunnel should be completed and open for traffic some time in 1993.

At the time of writing the final route of TGV-Nord — or 'Liaison Rapide Paris-Brussels-Cologne/Amsterdam' as it is officially described — has not yet been finalised but its main outline is known. Five different scenarios have been considered, but the following route seems likely to be the preferred choice.

Below:
The projected route of the TGV Nord.

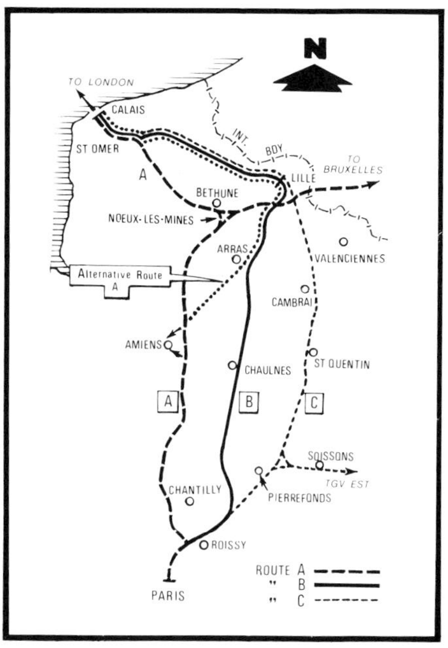

The new railway will start at Villiers le Bel, which is 16km (10 miles) out of Paris Nord, from where it will diverge to serve Roissy (Charles de Gaulle) International Airport. After Roissy the line will run through open country bypassing Arras which will be connected by a short branch to the existing railway network. At Lille — the only major French provincial centre on the route — there will be a triangular layout. This will provide: access between Paris, a new TGV station at Lille and the Channel Tunnel portal at Coquelles near Calais; a bypass line for trains between Paris, Belgium, Holland and the German Federal Republic not calling at Lille and a northern spur for trains between the Channel Tunnel, Lille, Belgium, Holland and the German Federal Republic.

After crossing the Belgian border at a point approximately 225km (140 miles) from Paris Nord, the line will pass through the town of Lembeek before joining existing SNCB (Belgian Railways) tracks into Brussels Midi station. The distance by the new line from Paris Nord to Brussels Midi is approximately 313km (194 miles).

The choice of route north and east of Brussels is a difficult decision. At one stage the Amsterdam and Cologne branches would have separated at Zaventem a few km north of Brussels Midi. The Amsterdam branch would have served Antwerp before passing into Holland where it will serve Rotterdam Schipol Airport and Amsterdam. The Cologne branch was to have run eastwards to serve either Liège or Aachen. However, to minimise environmental disturbance it now looks as if Belgium will omit both Antwerp and Liège and take the railway on a course to Herentals where the Amsterdam and Cologne routes would part company on a triangular layout which would also enable the Netherlands Railway (NS) to combine their Amsterdam-Cologne traffic with that from Brussels and Paris.

Channel Tunnel: an opportunity for BR

With BR connected physically to the European rail network the opportunities for through working — given that stock built to fit the restricted British loading gauge is available in sufficient numbers — are limitless. Now that the Anglo French Fixed Link Treaty has passed on to the Statute Book, BR's plans for the Channel Tunnel are now starting to gain momentum.

Leaving aside the car ferry trains and international freight services which will be a very important source of revenue for the tunnel owners, BR envisage a basic international service of trains between London and Paris in 3¼hr and London and Brussels in 3hr. These services will be provided by specially designed high-speed trains conforming to the British loading gauge but capable of working at speeds of up to 300km/hr on the European side of the Channel. These trains will also be equipped for operating over the SR 750V dc third-rail system between the tunnel and the London terminal station at Waterloo.

The Channel Tunnel poses a major challenge for BR. Superimposing additional 160km/hr (100mph) Channel Tunnel international expresses on the SR lines between Dover and London — particularly during the peak periods — will be a major problem. A programme of track and resignalling works to upgrade the SR route from 90 to 100mph will be implemented. Major works to provide access from the South Eastern section into the main line terminal at Waterloo — as well as major works at the station itself — will be necessary.

Extension of TGV-PSE

All the TGV projects described so far have been completely new, but the proposed extension of TGV-PSE northwards to a point closer to the Gare de Lyon in Paris and southwards to Marseille is even more interesting. The key to the Marseille extension is the synergy factor. We have already seen the impact of the *Ligne à Grande Vitesse* plus 200km/hr (125mph) speeds on the Paris, Rhône Valley and Montpellier/Marseille business but this pales by comparison with what SNCF now has in mind.

Below:
If plans for a European high speed network mature, it will be possible to travel from London, Cologne or Amsterdam to the southwest, southeast and west of France by TGV.

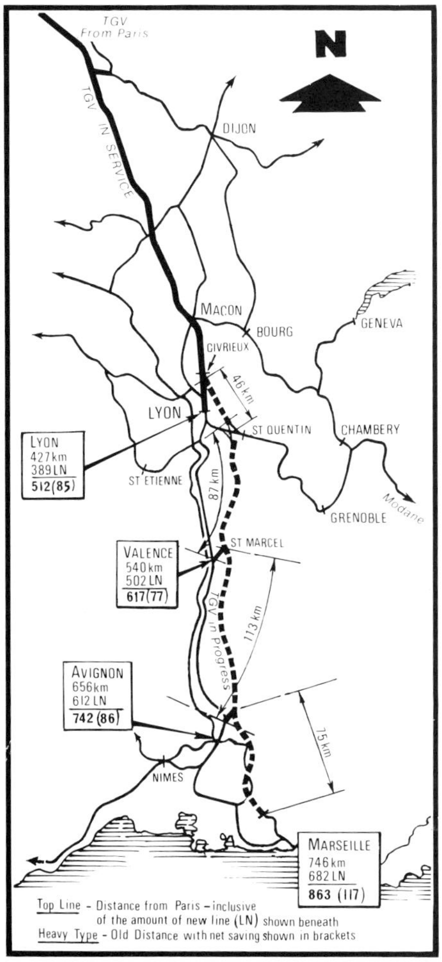

While the longer-term objective of the southern extension is to take the TGV to the Mediterranean coast, a more immediate aim is to provide TGV and ordinary rail facilities at Lyon Satolas International Airport for the 1992 Winter Olympics to be staged at various centres in the French Alps. Overseas visitors will fly in to Satolas and then use rail to reach the Games. The first section of the extension starts at Sathonay and follows a route to the new TGV airport station. The new Satolas station will also be used by ordinary trains between Satolas and Grenoble, Chambéry and other Alpine railheads. From Satolas the new line passes through open country where it will meet the existing Lyon to Grenoble/Chambéry line near the village of St Quentin. TGVs from Paris and ordinary trains from Satolas to Grenoble/Chambéry will leave the new line here and trains southbound from Lyon to Marseille will join the new line. The next section will be the 87km (54 miles) from St Quentin to St Marcel. At St Marcel a spur will make a connection to join the PLM classic route just north of Valence. St Marcel to Bedarrides, the third section, will be 113km (70 miles) long and will finish just south of Orange where there is a connection to the PLM line. This important connection will take TGVs to Avignon thence to Nimes, Montpellier, Perpignan and Port Bou. The final section will be the 75km (47 miles) from Bedarrides to Berre, the important industrial complex on the northern outskirts of Marseille.

Preliminary plans for the northern extension of the PSE high-speed line provide for about 30km (19 miles) of new railway which will take the existing line on an alignment which will join the existing network north of Villeneuve St Georges. As well as bringing the start of the high-speed line much closer to the centre of Paris, the new route will eliminate the present speed restriction over the existing lines between Villeneuve St Georges and Yerres; maximum speed will then be achieved only 10km (6 miles) out of the Gare de Lyon instead of at Lieusaint which is 29km (18 miles) from the Gare de Lyon.

Before looking at the new journey opportunities, it is necessary to mention that an important modification will be made to the PSE fleet by the time these extensions are built. By the start of the 1990s the PSE units will be due for a mid-life refurbishment when they will be re-equipped with synchronous motors enabling their maximum speed to be raised from 270 to 300km/hr (168

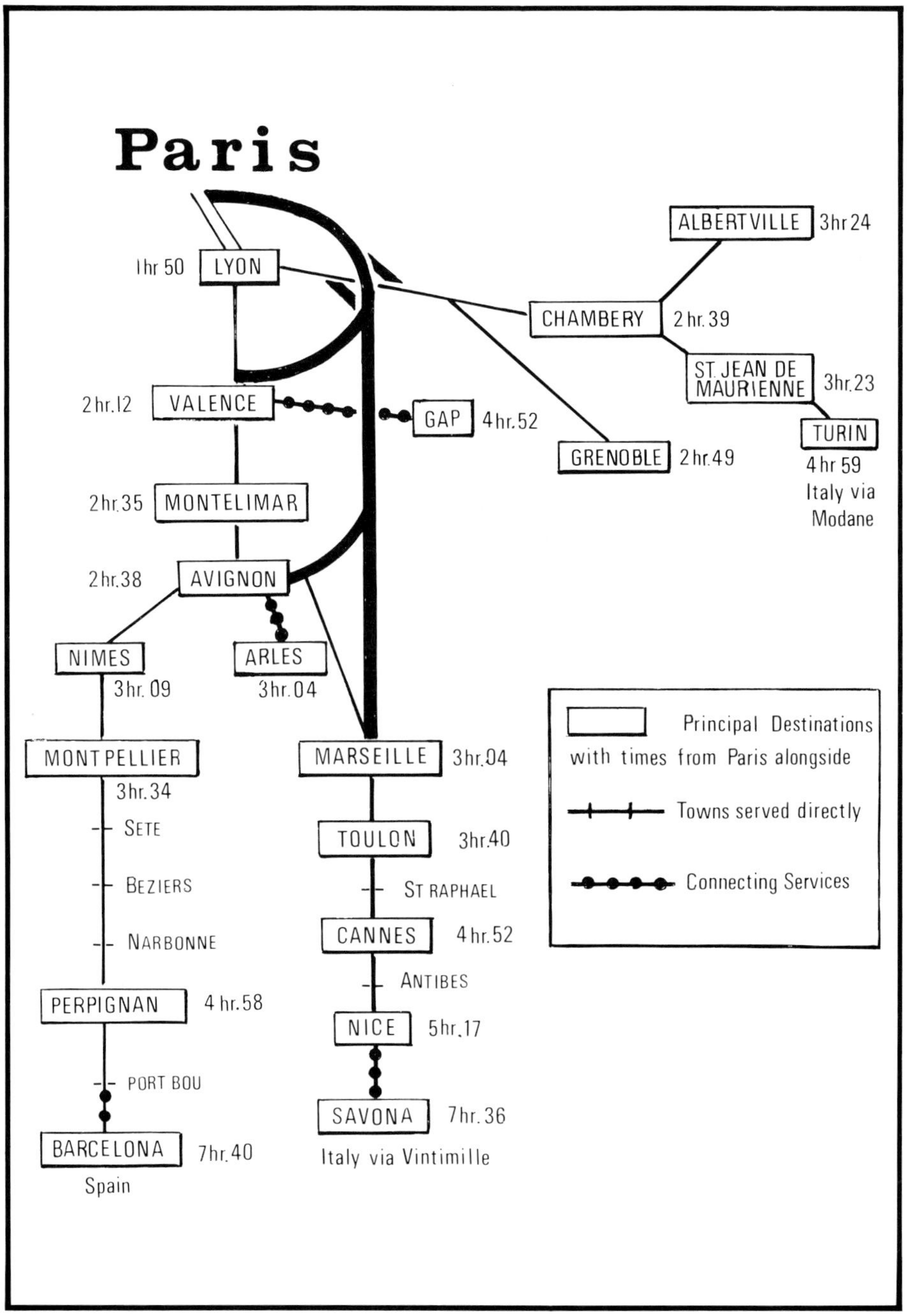

Above:
Anticipated journey times over the LGV-PSE extension to Marseille.

to 186mph). The adjacent map shows the exciting new range of journey opportunities, the highlights of which are:

(1) Journey time between Paris and Lyon is reduced by 10min from 2hr to 1hr 50min — an average speed of 233km/hr (144mph).
(2) Trains to and from Paris and Grenoble and Chambéry will benefit to a considerable degree by using the extension as far as St Quentin where they will diverge on to the Lyon-Grenoble/Chambéry line. Given a shorter distance and a much faster railway, Grenoble trains will avoid the long detour through the Lyon area and Chambéry trains will avoid the slow section from Ambérieu through the Alps. This new cut-off will also open up the possibility of routeing services to Italy through the Modane Tunnel to Turin and thence to Florence and on to the Florence-Rome high-speed *Dirrettissima*.
(3) Journey times between Paris and Avignon will be reduced to 2hr 38min and 3hr 34min to Montpellier. Given these reduced times it will now be worthwhile to extend TGV services beyond Montpellier to Perpignan and Port Bou. With a change at Port Bou, a time of just 7hr 40min between Paris and Barcelona looks possible.
(4) A journey time of just over 3hr between Paris and Marseille is particularly significant because it now brings this market, with its good baseload of business travel, within the 3hr threshold where centre-to-centre journey times by rail are faster than those by air.

If the go ahead is given the first stage from Sathonay to St Quentin (and possibly Valence) could be completed for the 1992 Winter Olympics, but the mid-1990s is a likely target for the complete extension to Marseille. Incidentally, the internal rate of return for the Sud Est extension is higher than SNCF's participation in their share of TGV-Nord. Similarly, no date has been set for the extension northwards into the Paris area and the link up with the TGV-Nord which is discussed below.

TGV-Est

Although plans for two alternative TGV-Est routes linking Paris and Strasbourg have been published, compared with other TGV projects the Est line has a low rate of return. Consequently, it has a low priority in SNCF's long-term plans. There are two alternative routes. The first route totalling 384km would serve Reims, Metz and Sarrebruck while the southerly route totalling 375km would only serve Nancy.

Paris TGV inter-connection

At one stage SNCF considered serving Roissy Airport by a loop off TGV-Nord. However, TGV-Nord will now be routed directly to Roissy as part of a TGV inter-connection system in the Paris outer area. As can be seen from the plan, a connection from TGV-PSE would run northeast to serve a new station located at the proposed Disneyland site, making a junction with a proposed TGV-Est from where it would join the TGV-Nord. Trains from North West Europe (London, Amsterdam, Brussels, Cologne) to the south of France would be able to bypass Paris. Access between TGV-Atlantique and TGV-Nord will be through Massy-Palaiseau, Valenton and Gagny on the existing Grande Ceinture network.

Below:
Map illustrating the potential interconnection of TGV routes in the Paris area.

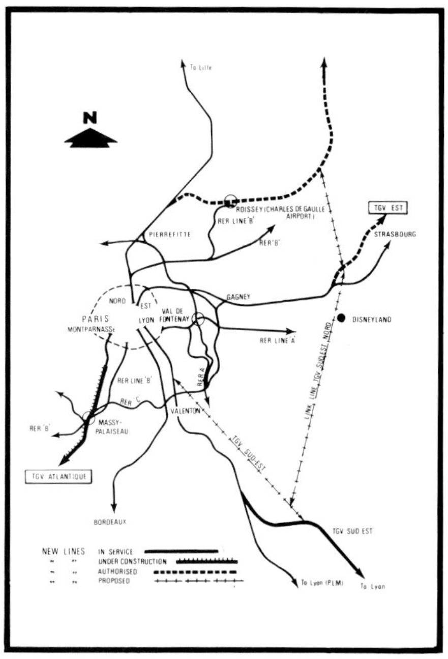

7.

The Paris-Sud Est Trains

As can be seen from the illustrations, the trains, which are finished in the now familiar brilliant red-orange livery, have an imposing appearance. Their looks are as good as their performance. Each train comprises two power cars and eight articulated trailers; the power cars can be detached, but the eight passenger cars are permanently coupled and can be lifted off their bogies only as a complete unit. To give the necessary power and speed, each 2+8 set has six motor bogies — two on each power car and one on the outer end of each of the

Right:
The PSE trains were designed with maximum seating capacity — they are functional but comfortable. Each Second Class coach seats 60 passengers with unidirectional seating throughout, with the exception of the central seats which are fitted face-to-face. *SNCF/CAV*

Below:
A TGV unit at full speed in open country. Each PSE unit has six traction motors — two are under each power car and one under each leading or trailing passenger vehicle. *SNCF/Fabbro*

Above:
First Class seating is in the standard 2+1 layout with 38 seats in a basic vehicle. Seating is unidirectional with a face-to-face arrangement in the centre.
SNCF/Dewolf

two adjacent vehicles in each eight-car rake. When running under 25kV ac on the LGV, the two power cars in each set can produce a combined output of 8,646hp; output under 1,500V dc and 16⅔Hz is lower. Power-to-weight ratio is very high at 22.4hp/tonne. There is a power line which runs along the roof of each set which passes the 25kV current to the rear power car. For multiple-unit working the nose-end of each power car opens to release the automatic coupler. All units can work in multiple.

There are four different TGV versions (see table 6). Of the standard version, offering both First and Second Class accommodation — there are 92 dual and eight triple-voltage sets, nine First Class-only dual-voltage sets and two postal sets. The nine First Class sets are used to strengthen peak hour services used by businessmen to and from Paris and Lyon. The 100 two-class sets each comprise three First Class cars, a bar car with 35 Second Class seats, and four Second Class cars. Baggage is stored in the leading First Class and rear Second Class vehicle. Space is provided for handicapped passengers.

Aircraft-style catering methods are the norm. Two serving points — for reheating food — are provided in the

passenger comfort. The pneumatic suspension designed for the Atlantique fleet is to be introduced in the PSE trains — 20 or so units will be converted each year through to 1990. To meet public criticism the bar area is to be expanded. The 35 existing seating places in the bar are to be removed so that the entire coach can be used as an expanded bar and lounge. Increased storage space will be provided so that a wider range of food and drink can be sold. Bar car conversions started in 1987 and will continue at the rate of 30 modifications per year until the entire fleet has been converted.

Mention should also be made of SNCF's plans for a mid-life refurbishment of the PSE fleet planned for the 1990s. The original motors will be replaced by synchronous traction motors. Fewer motors will be required which will reduce maintenance costs and traction current consumption. The maximum speed of the PSE fleet will be raised from 270 to 300km/hr.

Left:
Breakfast service in First Class.

first two First Class vehicles; a buffet serves all other passengers not taking full meals. By comparison with normal SNCF stock — and even with BR's smaller vehicles — the interior of the TGV is small, but acceptably so. In some respects it resembles an aircraft.

As the bulk of the business on the PSE line consists of passengers making the 2hr journey between Paris and Lyon, the trains were designed with a view to maximising seating rather than comfort. Whilst the trains are perfectly comfortable, the overall impression is functional. However, to maintain business, TGV services have been extended beyond the original network proposed when the project was planned. The new service between Paris and Nice will take about 7hr. With this in mind SNCF has studied a programme of modification to improve

Below:
Tray meal service in Second Class.

Right:
Another view of the original design of TGV Bar — the present cramped layout is to be expanded as units pass through the main works for overhaul.

Below right:
On Thursday 26 February 1981 a new World rail speed record was set by a TGV unit which achieved 236mph (380km/hr) at Pasilly (Yonne). *SNCF/CAV*

8.

Paris-Sud Est Signalling

TGV-PSE trains are equipped with special cab signalling for the LGV, the standard SNCF system for other parts of the network plus an additional aid for running at 200km/hr where this is authorised over certain sections of the Rhône Valley main line. The eight three-voltage 'Swiss' sets are also equipped with the Swiss Railway's 'Integra' cab warning system.

While the LGV signalling is fully automated, control of the train remains with the driver unless he ignores the cab indications in which case the brakes are applied automatically. The LGV is divided into block sections of 2.1km, but there are no conventional lineside signals. Instead, the block sections are shown by marker boards. A digital display in the drivers cab shows a maximum speed at which the train can pass the next marker board; any variation in the state of the line ahead is immediately shown on the display and

Below:
TGVs are equipped with a number of safety devices and are normally single-manned. The wheel in the centre of this cab layout is the main power controller which incorporates a vigilance device which, if released, will apply the brakes to the train. Note the radio telephone communication with the main Paris Control Centre. *SNCF*

Below right:
Satellite signal relay post at Vaux en Pre at KP293. Note the high-speed cross-over. *SNCF/CAV*

— if it is more restrictive than the speed at which the train is travelling — a warning signal sounds in the cab advising the driver to reduce speed. There are two types of lineside marker boards — 'F' (*Franchissable*) and 'Nf' (*Non-franchissable*). 'F' boards can be passed under stop-and-proceed rules, but Nf boards have an absolute stop status. The signalling can handle trains at 4min headways; 270km/hr is the maximum permitted speed but the equipment is capable of signalling trains at 300km/hr.

When five or more block sections ahead are clear, the cab display shows the letters VL (*Voie Libre*) or line clear. If only four sections ahead are clear the display will show 270; in this case the driver can pass the next marker board at 270km/hr but it is a warning that he may have to reduce speed at the next marker. Warnings to reduce speed at subsequent marker boards will appear on the digital display as 220, 160 and 000. Three zeros tells the driver that he must stop at the next marker board, but there will still be a block section between his train and the next occupied section ahead. If a driver overshoots the marker board three red rectangles appear on the cab display.

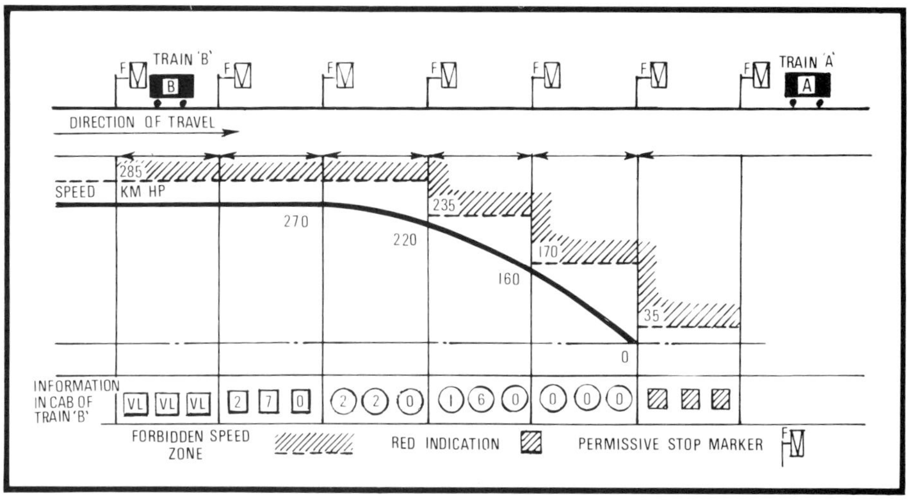

Left:
Diagram showing the in-cab signals as one train ('B') approaches another stationary one ('A') on the LGV. With five clear sections in-between, the driver is told 'Voie Libre'; as he gets nearer the obstruction the safe speed drops appropriately.

Far left:
A close-up view of a high-speed cross-over. *SNCF/CAV*

Left:
A Nf marker board; note the gradient.

Below left:
F signal and marker board at KP280 south of Le Creusot station. *SNCF/CAV*

Below:
Close-up view of a Nf marker board.

9.

The Postal TGVs

A little-known feature of TGV PSE is the existence of the small fleet of two purpose-built TGV postal trains which carry PTT (French Post Office) traffic between Paris and Lyon. As the PSE project began to take shape, the PTT became interested in the possibility of using the TGV for their carriage of postal traffic — thus continuing the long-standing arrangement with SNCF for the carriage of mails in special PTT stock. Agreement was reached whereby PTT would finance the construction of 2½ TGV sets. The Postal TGVs which started service on 1 October 1984, replaced an overnight air service between Paris and Lyon provided by two Transall 160 aircraft. The payload of a Postal TGV set is 88 tonnes (176 tonnes if working in multiple) compared with 14.3 tonnes on the Transall 160. Technically the postal sets are identical to the passenger fleet, but there are no windows, passenger doors or seats. Internally there is space for the storage of trolleys covering sacks of mail and parcels etc; access is through a door in the side of each vehicle. The two sets are painted in the standard PTT yellow and grey livery. To provide cover for

maintenance, postal trains are built as half sets (a power car plus four articulated coaches) which are numbered from 1 to 5.

The Postal TGVs are part of a complex PTT distribution network covering the whole of South East France involving air, road and SNCF services. At Mâcon and Lyon the trains transfer traffic and make connections with other postal services covering the rest of the network. There are two Postal TGV services in each direction (see table) between Paris-Charolais (the postal depot adjoining the Gare de Lyon) and Lyon-Montrochet which is on the west side of the Lyon area complex. Mâcon-Vinzelles postal station is located on the single line connection between the LGV and PLM lines at Mâcon. To avoid reversal the north and south-bound Postal TGVs serving Mâcon Vinzelles use the PLM line between Creches-sur-Saône and Lyon Montrochet (see plan).

Table 10: TGV PSE Postal Train Workings

Southbound

Train No		1	2
Paris-Charolais	*(dep)*	19.41	22.30
Mâcon-Vinzelles	*(arr)*	—	00.27
	(dep)	—	00.37
Lyon-Montrochet	*(arr)*	22.08	01.13

Northbound

Train No		3	4
Lyon Montrochet	*(dep)*	09.44	23.25
Mâcon-Vinzelles	*(arr)*	—	00.03
	(dep)	—	00.13
Paris Charolais	*(arr)*	12.19	02.25

Notes:
(i) After arrival at Lyon Montrochet, train 1 returns to Paris, departing at 23.25.
(ii) Trains 1, 2 and 4 use the LGV between Lieusaint and Mâcon and the PLM through Crêche-sur-Saône to Lyon.
(iii) Train 4 runs from Lyon Montrochet to Paris via Lyon Part-Dieu, Sathnay and the LGV.

Below left:
Postal TGV arriving at Paris with mail from Lyon. *David Haydock*

Below:
The Postal TGV route network.

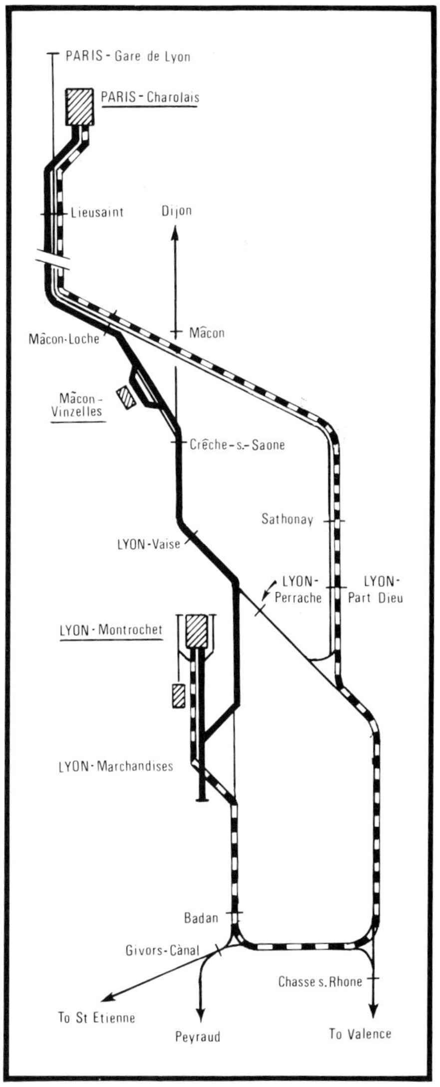

APPENDIX 1
The TGV Units

Basic Specification

Table 11

Details	*TGV-PSE*	*TGV-A*
Power Cars:	2	2
Trailers: First Class	3	3
Second Class	6	6
Buffet	*	1
Formation†	2+8	2+10
Seating: First Class	111	116
Second Class	275	369
Total	386	485
Power:	8,646hp	8,579hp
Weight:	386 tonnes	490 tonnes
Power/Weight Ratio:	22.40	19.32
Maximum Service Speed:	270km/hr (168mph)	300km/hr (186mph)
Length:	200.19m	237.56m
Number of Sets:	109	97

* Buffet facilities are installed in a Second Class vehicles in PSE sets.
† Refers to standard sets only. There are also nine all-First sets.

General Description

Formation: Two power cars enclosing trailers forming an articulated and permanently-coupled unit.

Main Characteristics: Overall length 200.19m. Wheelsets — two bogies with two motored axles to each motor unit and one on each adjoining trailer. Seven bogies under the articulation and inter-communication rings of the trailers.

Traction Equipment

Power Cars
One single-phase pantograph, one dc pantograph, 25kV supply line, single-phase dc circuit breaker, transformer — all roof-mounted. Internally fitted main transformer and self-induction coils, dc circuit breaker, independent traction installation unit and rheostatic braking equipment for each group of two motors (one to each of the motor bogies and one for the motor bogie of the adjoining trailers). Batteries carried on underframe

End trailers
Static convertor of 400kVA for three-phase 380V feed to auxiliaries and trainset air-conditioning groups.
25kV supply line (roof-mounted) and isolating switch.
Intermediate trailers
Roof-mounted 25kV supply line.
Equipment for multiple operation of two sets.

Driving and Safety Aids

Imposed speed; anti-skid device; automatic supervision; interphone; radio link; cab signalling (11 continuous speed indications and five for punctuality, speed control); signal repeaters, and advance warning system for standard SNCF network.

Bodies

Bodywork bodyframe forming a tubular girder structure, plated in semi-stainless steel, glass and polyester. Electric auto-coupler between two trainsets; classic coupler between motor units and outermost trailers.

Interior Layout

Folding/sliding access doors with automatic opening and closing; inter-vehicle gangway connection with mobile lower plate. Automatic inter-communicating doors open and close simultaneously on adjoining ends of consecutive trailers. Automatically operated saloon doors. Double-glazed fixed windows with laminated, semi-reflective outer panes and tempered inner panes. Four windows to each body, of which two may be secured, are double-glazed, wholly-tempered and may be used as emergency exits. Retention-type toilets. Central sound-proofing in middle of set; independent installation for the bar; special interphone for use between driving cabs and guard's compartment.

Bogies and Suspension

Mechanically-welded frame; drive by spindle (type 230 motor bogies) or floating pivot (type 231); axleboxes and cartridge-type roller bearings. Primary suspension by rubber studs and spiral springs. Secondary suspension by spiral springs. Vertical, transverse and looped hydraulic shock absorbers.

Braking

Rheostatic. Each bogie brake is independent of the others. High power automatic air brake, with electro-pneumatic control. Double cast iron shoes on all wheels and two double discs on each carrying axle. Automatic immobilisation brake on motor bogies.

Air Conditioning

Cab air conditioning group in power cars. Compression refrigeration equipment of 25,000kcal in trailers. Heating equipment in saloon 30kW; in vestibule 1,250kW×2; in toilets 1kW; distribution of conditioned air — 3,000m^3/hr.

Numbering

Power cars are numbered from 23001 (two-voltage units) and 33001 (three-voltage units); the number of each vehicle is preceded by the letters TGV and, for the trailers, symbols, series letters and characteristic passenger stock indices: 2r or R, A, B, D, r, u etc.

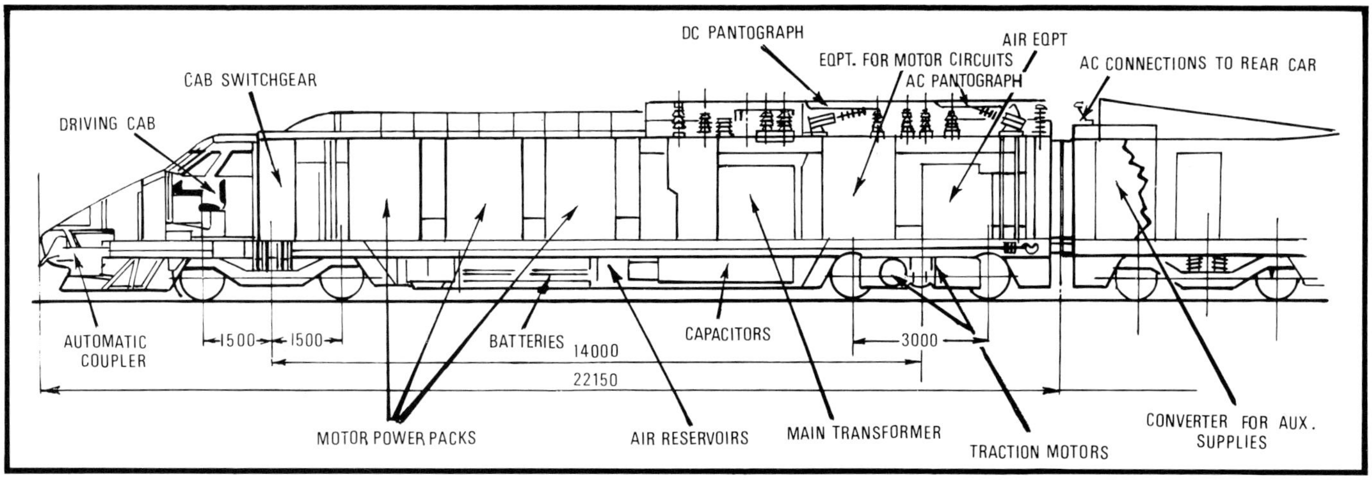

The trailers bear a six-figure number. The first one from the left (1-8) indicates the position of the trailer from the first motor unit in the set. The following two figures indicate that it belongs to a two- or three-voltage set. The last three on the right indicate the number of the set (carried at each end on motor units).

Probably because the successful launch of TGV coincided with the demise of British Rail's Advanced Passenger Train (APT), the two projects have often been compared. The APT was a revolutionary concept which included a host of technical innovations, but the TGV design is based on proven technology. Essentially APT was a new design to run on an old railway whereas TGV was part of a total project including a purpose-built railway.

An important mechanical feature of the TGV is that the eight trailers of the basic 10-car set are articulated, one bogie supporting the ends of two coaches throughout. The power cars, one at each end of the set, are not articulated with the trailers, and there are only 13 bogies in the 10-car train instead of 20. The big decrease in train resistance reduces the energy consumption of a TGV by 30% compared with a conventional locomotive-hauled train.

The total power output of a TGV running on 25kV ac is 6,300kW (8,448hp) from 12 traction motors. If motors large enough to provide such an output were carried only on the two power cars, the axle-load would be too great, so there are six two-axle motor bogies in the train, two under each power car and one under the outer end (next to the power car) of the first and last trailers. This arrangement reduces track wear.

The LGV-PSE is fed at 25kV ac. For all journeys, therefore, TGVs have to use two-voltages. Maximum speed on the high-speed line is 270km/hr (167.78mph) but on other lines they must conform to existing speed limits of 200 or 160km/hr (125 or 100mph).

SNCF has a large fleet of ac/dc locomotives, for which dc control by chopper is now favoured, the chopper being fed direct from the contact wire on 1,500V dc or through a transformer/rectifier set giving 1,500V dc output when running on 25kV ac. The chopper provides smooth electronic control of traction motor voltage without loss of energy in resistances. Although the chopper system is used for control of the TGV on dc, the control on ac is by a conventional thyristor system similar to that fitted to the recent series of BR EMUs.

If a chopper had been used by itself, a fault in the transformer/rectifier could have put all motors of a power car out of action. In the TGV installation, every motor bogie has its own power pack, connected to its own transformer winding. It is most unlikely that more than one power pack would fail at a given time, but even with two out of action a TGV can start and accelerate on the steepest LGV gradients (nearly 1 in 28).

Each power car is equipped with one ac and one dc pantograph. With an ac pantograph raised at the front and rear of the train, there could be problems in current collection on the rear power car because of vibrations in the contact wire set from the leading car. Only one pantograph per unit is therefore used on ac and power is fed from it to the second power car through a 25kV cable laid along the vehicle roofs.

An unusual method of mounting the traction motors has been adopted in order to minimise unsprung weight on the motor bogies. Normally, traction motors are attached to the bogie frames, but on the TGV the motors and gearcases are carried by cross-members on the underside of the car body. This has made a special form of cardan shaft drive necessary. The shaft is coupled at one end by a universal joint to the gearbox on the motor, and at the other end there is a similar coupling to another gearbox, supported

Above:
Layout of a TGV power unit.

Below:
Cut-away view of TGV vehicle articulation.

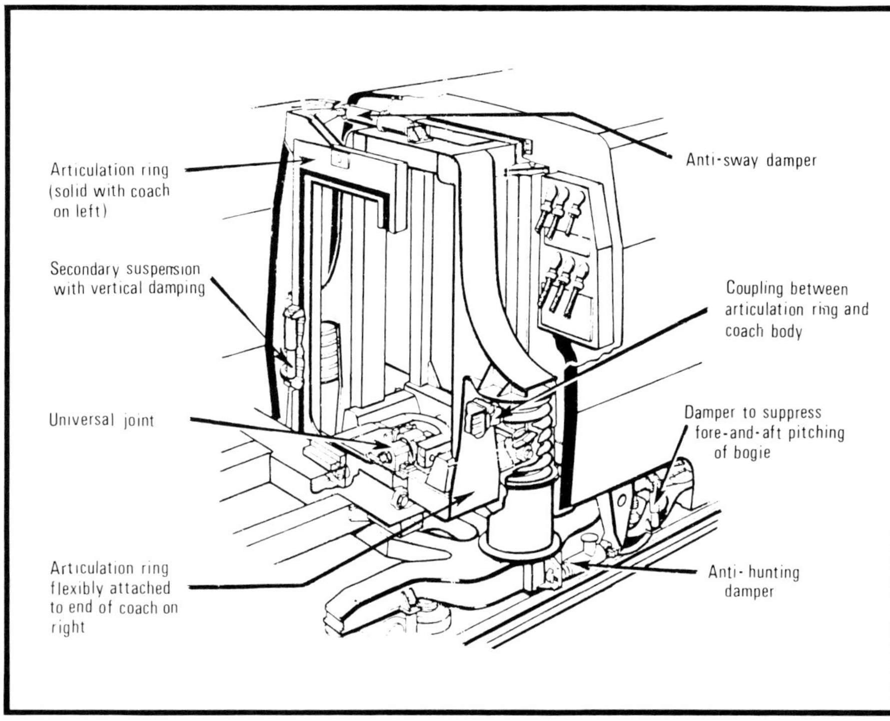

by the axle and housing the final drive. A telescopic joint is incorporated in the shaft, which can extend or shorten as necessary to allow for sideways movements of the bogie relative to the body.

The coupling between the end trailers and the power cars takes the usual buffer and drawgear form so that the whole rake of eight trailers can be easily uncoupled. A special form of coupling is used between trailers. The connection is formed by two oval rings through which passengers can pass when moving up and down the train. Provision is made for separating trailers when necessary for maintenance. This type of articulation provides a low floor level, with easier passenger access, and a reduced train height of 3.42m from rail level to roof, compared with 4.05m in other modern rolling stock. A result is lower air resistance at high speeds, the area exposed being 12% less.

There are three braking systems: rheostatic on the power cars, disc brakes and brake blocks on the trailers (brake blocks also act on the power car wheels below 160km/hr). In rheostatic braking, the power car motors are separately excited from batteries via a chopper. The braking resistors are fixed in value but their effective resistance is varied electronically to control the braking effort.

Provision has been made for multiple unit operation. Couplers which also carry the control cables are built into the front ends of the power cars and are concealed by shutters when not in use. The 25kV power cable is not connected between sets and so each collects current from one of its own pantographs. Fears that the leading pantograph might disturb current collection on the rear set proved to be unfounded.

Below:
Two TGV units in multiple, showing the coupler apertures in the vehicle ends.
SNCF

Bottom:
TGV stopping distances.

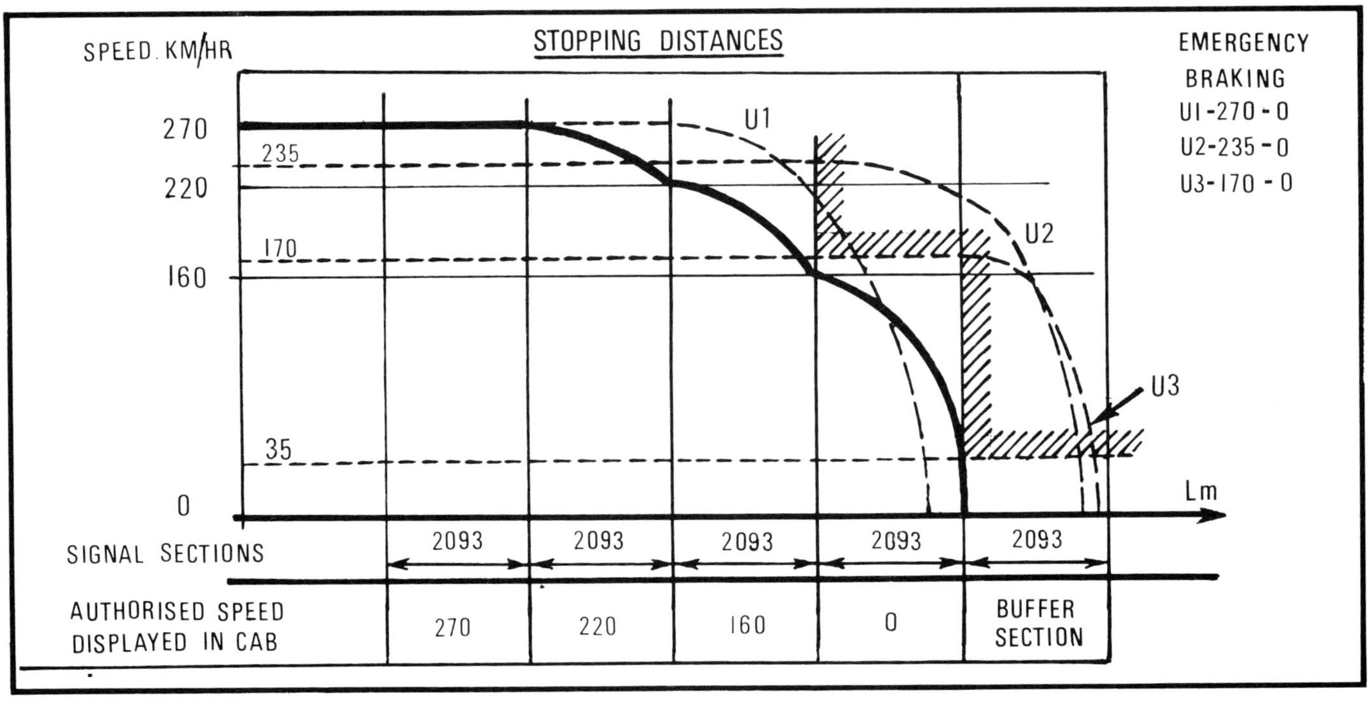

APPENDIX 2

TGV Performance

By Peter Barlow

With such frequent and sharp changes in gradient, TGV speeds are virtually impossible to record and are often not really meaningful. However, times together with average speeds, enable one run to be compared sensibly with another. By taking split times at every km post during speed build up on the new line one can, if one wishes, plot the relative acceleration to line speed. (NB: km posts are on the east side.) Because schedules have so much reserve a flat-out run is very rare and is most likely northbound if there is a significantly late start from Lyon. The tendency is for power to be off for a considerable time when changing voltage entering the new line which is followed by a full power acceleration up to line speed. Thereafter the speed selection device is usually set at a level which restricts early running to say, 230 or 240km/hr. The driver checks his time against his schedule at every relay room (PRS) and sometimes a higher speed is needed later in the run in order to enter back on to the ordinary railway with 1 or 2min in hand.

Influences on speed

Because of vertical curvature there are restrictions to 220km/hr at several summits, 220km/hr being the next speed level below line maximum in the automatic surveillance device. In practice speed will fall away on its own accord to about 220km/hr up the steepest gradients, but on occasions electronic braking can be felt just before the top of a bank is reached. Neutral sections along the route also cause the speed to drop especially where located on a rising gradient. Drivers often prefer to work in the manual driving mode to make the task more interesting, so fluctuations in speed tend to be unpredictable. The three logs illustrate typical TGV performance each with features of its own.

This was a special run for members of the Institution of Railway Signal Engineers and was designed to show off the capabilities of the TGV train and the signalling system. Hence it was run at maximum speed over the whole length of the new line albeit at that time only the southern section and still at 260km/hr. Thus the section from Carisey to Les Muenieres (the first and last point where 260km/hr running was possible) was run at 158.7mph (256.4km/hr) — a near perfect performance.

Table 12: Special TGV 601: 10.52 Paris-Lyon Brotteaux, 25 May 1983
Set 75

Miles		*Sch*	*min sec*	*mph average*
0.00	PARIS Gare de Lyon	0	0 00	(1 late)
2.50	Charenton		4 18	
8.95	Villeneuve St Georges	9	11 09	
16.10	Combs la Ville		16 31	79.9
27.40	MELUN	23	23 41	94.6
36.60	Fontainebleau		29 30	94.9
41.50	Moret		32 34	95.9
48.85	MONTEREAU	37	37 16	93.8
			sigs	85.5
62.95	Pont sur Yonne		47 10	
69.95	SENS	51	51 44	92.0
78.90	Villeneuve sur Yonne		57 32	92.6
90.40	Joigny		65 01	92.2
96.25	LAROCHE	68	68 48	92.8
			eased	80.3
101.60	Brienon		72 48	
105.95	Vergigny	76	76 15	75.7
	KM118.3			134.3
112.85	Carisey		79 20	
119.30	Tonnerre		81 46	159.0
133.15	Pasilly	89	87 00	158.8
145.60	Toutry		91 36	162.4
158.20	Lacour D'Arcenay		96 21	159.2
172.75	Vianges	105	101 48	160.2
186.15	Sully		106 47	161.3
202.55	LE CREUSOT TGV	117	112 58	159.1
214.50	Vaux En Pré		117 42	151.5*
227.30	Cluny		122 36	156.7*
239.95	MÂCON TGV	132	127 31	154.4*
256.80	Cesseins		133 51	159.6
266.90	Les Meunièrses		137 35	162.3
			sigs	88.2
274.35	Sathonay	148	142 39	
274.50	Signal C.31		143 31	sig stop
			148 06	
277.50	St Clair		153 34	
279.10	LYON BROTTEAUX	157	156 04	(Time)

* 3 summits (220km/h limit)
255km/hr by Carisey
Start to stop average: 107.3mph (172.6km/hr)

This was positively the first advertised public run on fast timings over the whole route in the southbound direction, although there had been impromptu runs in the previous days. Diversions to secondary tracks in the Paris suburban area for planned engineering works meant there was a 3min late entry on to the new line and hence running at line maximum continued as far as Le Creusot by which time the train was running 2min early. Between Jard (where there is an obscure traction switching hut that is recognisable in darkness at a point where acceleration is complete) and Le Creusot the pass-to-pass average was 264km/hr (164.1mph) which is about as close to the 270km/hr ceiling as can be achieved, given the fluctuations in speed already described. Power was reduced after Le Creusot and Lyon Part-Dieu was reached 1min early, passing slowly through the old Brotteaux station which had been closed only the previous day. Net time was about 118min, but note that the actual distance travelled on this run was 0.4 miles more than the normal distance in the southbound direction. This is because the slow tracks, and also the northbound fast track, in the area of Villeneuve-St-Georges, sweeps round an enormous curve to create a flying junction.

Table 13: TGV 603 0700 Paris-Lyon Perrache 25 September 1983

Set 32

Miles		*Sch*	*min*	*sec*	*mph average*	
0.00	PARIS Gare de Lyon	0	0	00	31.3	(Time)
2.50	Charenton		4	48		
			sigs		64.1	
8.95	Villeneuve St Georges	8½	10	50	70.9	
13.50	Brunoy		14	41		
			sigs		78.6	
19.35	Lieusaint	15½	19	09	109.0	(−3½)
24.80	Jard		22	09	164.3	
34.75	Châtelet en Brie	22	25	47	166.8	
49.30	Marolles	28	31	01	165.6	(−3)
63.10	Cuy	33½	36	01	161.1	
76.35	Vaumort	39	40	57	160.3	
92.20	Verigny	45	46	53		(−2)
	KM118.3				165.7	
105.55	Tonnerre	50½	51	43	163.5	
119.40	Pasilly	56	56	48	167.2	
131.80	Toutry	61	61	15	163.8	
144.45	Lacour D'Arcenay	66½	65	53	164.7	(+½)
158.95	Vianges	72½	71	10	167.5	
172.40	Sully	78	75	59	160.4	
188.80	LE CREUSOT TGV	84½	82	07	142.0	(+2½)
200.75	Vaux En Pré	89½	87	10	147.2	
213.55	Cluny	94½	92	23	140.1	
226.20	MÂCON TGV	99½	97	48	144.8	(+1½)
243.05	Cesseins	106½	104	47	146.5	
253.10	Les Meunières		108	54	96.8	
260.55	Sathonay	115½	113	31	56.7	(+2)
263.75	St Clair	119½	116	54	40.0	
265.35	Lyon Brotteaux		119	18	18.9	
265.85	LYON PART DIEU	122	120	53		(+1)

Start to stop average: 131.9mph (212.26km/hr)

Summer 1984 was the first timetable to allow 200km/hr speeds off the new line for a total of some 70 miles in two sections either side of Avignon. Whilst not fully exploited on this run because the train was on time, the result is a start-to-stop average of 93.7mph from Valence to Avignon and 90.0mph from Avignon to Marseille. These are considerably above what is possible with the normal 160km/hr (100mph) limit, particularly bearing in mind the much lower speeds permitted over the last 20 or so miles into Marseille.

Table 14: TGV 815: 11.42 Paris-Marseille, 20 October 1984

Set 80 (Marseille) and **70** (Montpellier)

Miles		*Sch*	*min*	*sec*	*mph average*	
0.00	VALENCE	0	0	00	53.3	(−2)
3.6	Portes		4	03	97.8	
10.8	Lirron		8	28	98.3	
17.0	Saulee		12	15	99.4	
27.6	MONTELIMAR		18	39	97.3	
33.3	Châteauneuf du Rhône		22	10	96.6	
41.0	Pierrelatte		26	57	120.0	
48.2	Bollene		30	33	100.0	
59.9	ORANGE		37	34	111.8	
71.2	Sorgues		43	38		
			eased		62.2	
77.3	AVIGNON	51	49	31		(−½)
					59.2	(−½)
3.8	Barbentane		3	51	98.2	
7.7	Graveson		6	14	103.1	
13.6	Tarascon		9	40	117.5	
21.5	ARLES		13	42	116.5	
31.5	St Martin de Crau		18	51	105.3	
42.0	MIRAMAS		24	50	92.3	
54.0	Berre		32	38	91.9	
63.5	Pas des Lanciers		38	50	87.9	
70.9	St Louis		43	53	38.9	
74.8	MARSEILLE St Charles	51	49	54		(+½)

200km/h Pierrelatte-Miramas from 20.9.84
Start to stop averages: 93.7mph
90.0mph